Easy English!

Series Editor

Adrian Wallwork
English for Academics SAS
Pisa, Italy

Easy English is a series of books intended for students and teachers of English as a foreign language.

More information about this series at http://www.springer.com/series/15586

Adrian Wallwork

Top 50 Vocabulary Mistakes

How to Avoid Them

 Springer

Adrian Wallwork
English for Academics SAS
Pisa, Italy

ISSN 2522-8617 ISSN 2522-8625 (electronic)
Easy English!
ISBN 978-3-319-70980-2 ISBN 978-3-319-70981-9 (eBook)
https://doi.org/10.1007/978-3-319-70981-9

Library of Congress Control Number: 2017963154

© Springer International Publishing AG 2018
This work is subject to copyright. All rights are reserved by the Publisher, whether the whole or part of the material is concerned, specifically the rights of translation, reprinting, reuse of illustrations, recitation, broadcasting, reproduction on microfilms or in any other physical way, and transmission or information storage and retrieval, electronic adaptation, computer software, or by similar or dissimilar methodology now known or hereafter developed.
The use of general descriptive names, registered names, trademarks, service marks, etc. in this publication does not imply, even in the absence of a specific statement, that such names are exempt from the relevant protective laws and regulations and therefore free for general use.
The publisher, the authors and the editors are safe to assume that the advice and information in this book are believed to be true and accurate at the date of publication. Neither the publisher nor the authors or the editors give a warranty, express or implied, with respect to the material contained herein or for any errors or omissions that may have been made. The publisher remains neutral with regard to jurisdictional claims in published maps and institutional affiliations.

Printed on acid-free paper

This Springer imprint is published by Springer Nature
The registered company is Springer International Publishing AG
The registered company address is: Gewerbestrasse 11, 6330 Cham, Switzerland

Contents

Part I Top 50 Vocabulary Mistakes

1. According to 3
2. Actual, Actually 5
3. Advice, Advise 7
4. Agree 9
5. Among, Between, Of, From 11
6. Appreciate 13
7. As, Like 15
8. Available, Comfortable, Convenient 17
9. Beautiful, Good, Fine, Nice 21
10. Because, Why 23
11. Big, Great, Large 27
12. Borrow, Lend, Loan 31
13. Both, Either, Neither 33
14. Bring, Take, Carry, Fetch, Get, Lead 37
15. Camping, Campsite, Parking, Car Park 41
16. Chance, Possibility, Occasion 43
17. Close, Near, Next 47
18. Clothes, Dress, Dresses, Get Dressed, Put on, Wear ... 51
19. Come, Go 55
20. Control, Check 57

21	Cook, Cooker, Cooking, Kitchen, Dish, Course, Plate............	59
22	Do, Make	61
23	Early, Soon, On Time, In Time	63
24	Earn, Gain, Win, Beat, Deserve.............................	65
25	Economic, Economical, Economically, Financial................	67
26	Education, Background, Upbringing, (Good / Bad) Manners, Training	69
27	Enjoy, Have A Good Time, Funny, Fun	73
28	Enough, Quite, Pretty, Sufficient............................	75
29	Even If, Even Though, Although	79
30	Ever, Never, Always..	81
31	Expect, Wait (For)...	83
32	Find, Find Out, Discover, Search, Look For..................	87
33	Fit, Match, Suit, Go Well With	91
34	Grow, Grow Up, Increase, Cultivate.........................	93
35	Happen, Occur, Take Place	97
36	Home, House; Homework, Housework.......................	99
37	In the End, At the End, Eventually, Finally, At Last, Lastly, If Necessary	103
38	Job, Work..	107
39	Know, Meet	111
40	Last, Latest, Most Recent; Next, the Next	115
41	Look At, See, Watch	119
42	Look, Seem, Sound	121
43	Lose, Lack, Miss, Waste....................................	125
44	Remember, Remind, Forget.................................	129
45	Rise, Arise, Raise...	133
46	Say, Tell	135
47	Sorry, Excuse, Apologize	137
48	Think, Think Of, Think About, Believe	139
49	Travel, Trip, Way...	141

50	**Understand, Catch, Figure Out, Realize**............................	143

Part II Revision Tests

51	**Revision Tests**...	147

Part III False Friends

52	**False Friends**...	161
	Appendix...	167
	Index..	173

Student's Introduction

What Is Easy English?

Easy English is a series of books to help you learn and revise your English with minimal effort.

There are two main strands of the series. You can improve your English by

1. doing short exercises to improve specific areas of vocabulary (this book) and grammar. The grammar and vocabulary books focus on the areas that tend to lead to the most mistakes. The aim is just to highlight what you really need, rather than overwhelming you with a mass of rules, many of which may have no practical daily value
2. reading texts in English that you might well normally read in your own language (e.g. personality tests, jokes, lateral thinking games, word searches).

Who Is the Book for? What Level Do I Need to Be?

Anyone who is interested in eliminating the typical mistakes they make when faced between choosing from a set a of similar words.

You need to have reached a mid-intermediate level of English to benefit from this book.

How Many Vocabulary Mistakes Are Dealt with?

This book is called *The Top 50 Vocabulary Mistakes*. In reality there are over 150 words dealt within the 50 sections of Part I of this book. Another 50 false friends are dealt with, in less detail, in Part III.

How Is the Book Organized?

Each chapter has a HEADING which gives the key words dealt with in the section. In the explanations below I will be referring to Chapter 5 (*among, between, of, from*).

Each chapter is made up of five subsections.

1. THE FIRST SUBSECTION shows some typical mistakes. All sentences in *italics* are mistakes. Each mistake is then followed in the line below with the correct version (in normal script). The key point is highlighted in bold in the correct version. Here is an example:

   Many people can't distinguish among red and green.
   Many people can't distinguish **between** red and green.

   In the above example, the writer of the first sentence has incorrectly chosen *among* instead of *between*.

   Note that other typical mistakes where some languages use a different word from the key word, may also be listed in this subsection. For example,

   Illiteracy is commonest under rural women.
   Illiteracy is commonest **among** rural women.

   In the above example *under* has been used instead of *among*. However, the word *under* is not dealt with in the other three subsections. This is because it is not one of the keywords (*among, between, of*) in the heading of the section. It is simply mentioned to raise your awareness that in your language you may use a completely different word. Such mistakes are tested in the Revisions Tests in Part II of this book.

2. In the SECOND SUBSECTION correct examples are given of the key words used in typical situations. These correct examples are shown in a box with a grey background. Here is an example:

   > He was standing **between** Paul and Joseph.
   > She was standing **among** a crowd of hooligans.

3. In the THIRD SUBSECTION, very simple guidelines are given of the key words. For example:
   - **between** = two different items or groups of distinct items
   - **among** = a number of indistinct different items
   - **of** = before an indeterminate number of the same item
   - **from** = after a verb when making a selection (*choose from, pick from, select from*)

These guidelines are not comprehensive, they are designed to give you a quick easy-to-remember guideline to the most common uses of the particular word in question. For example, in the above case the use of *of* given is just one of many possible uses of *of*. It refers only to the use of *of* in relation to the use of *among* and *between*.

If you need more detailed explanations for the words, then I suggest you use an online dictionary (e.g. *Word Reference* or *The Cambridge Online Learners Dictionary*) or view the comments on various English forums where readers explain the differences between certain words.

4. In the FOURTH SUBSECTION, there is an exercise which tests the key words given in the heading of the chapter, so in this case *among, between, from* and *of*. A few of the exercises are based on exercises that can be found in *English for Academic Research: Vocabulary Exercises* (Springer), which is part of a series of books on academic English, whereas the book you are reading now is focused on general English.
5. The FINAL SUBSECTION is the key. Where there is space, I have given the full sentence containing the correct answer. Where there has not been sufficient space for the full sentence, I have just listed the correct word.

Level of English Used in the Tests

Most of the sentences used in the tests are authentic (i.e. real texts). A few come from academic tests and are thus quite formal, whereas the majority reflect the more neutral and informal aspects of English. Many of the more informal sentences are taken from movie scripts and thus reflect how English is spoken, not just written. One of my main sources was context.reverso.net, which is one of the most useful websites on the internet for reading real examples of English in use.

The idea for choosing authentic texts is to provide an alternative to the majority of vocabulary books where sentences are written specifically for non native readers.

This may mean that you encounter some unfamiliar expressions and vocabulary. I suggest two possible solutions:

1. ideally you should use an online dictionary to help you find the meanings. Again, you might find context.reverso.net to be the best solutions, as on this site typical phrases are found both in their English versions and in a multitude of other languages.
2. skip the difficult sentences. You will find that the vocabulary items are tested over several sentences, so if you skip a few because you don't have time to check any unknown vocabulary, then you will still be practising using the key words in context.

Revision Tests

In Part II of the book there is a revision test. This test deals with all the incorrect sentences given in the first subsections of each section. For example, *under*, which was not tested in the fourth subsection mentioned above, is tested here. These tests are essentially the list of the mistakes, but without the corrected version. Your job is to correct the sentences and then compare them with the relevant corrected versions in the relevant section.

False Friends

In the final part of the book (Part III), there are a few exercises on some typical false friends, i.e. an English word that may be spelt very similarly to a word in your language (and which probably derives from Latin or Greek) but which has a different meaning.

Where Can I Find More Grammar Explanations and Tests?

Top 50 Vocabulary Mistakes is aimed at students studying general English. I have also written a series of books on academic English.

If you want more detailed grammar explanations, then you can find them in this book:

English for Research: Grammar, Usage and Style https://link.springer.com/book/10.1007/978-1-4614-1593-0

If you would like to do extra vocabulary exercises and see examples of English sentences in a more technical context, then you can use this book:

English for Academic Research: Vocabulary Exercises https://link.springer.com/book/10.1007/978-1-4614-1593-0

The companion to *Top 50 vocabulary mistakes*, which is entitled *Top 50 Grammar Mistakes*, also contains many exercises that you might find useful.

By using all these books in combination, your level of English should improve considerably.

In the appendix, you can find the index to the *Grammar Exercises* and the Table of Contents of the *Vocabulary Exercises* book. This will help you to find additional grammar explanations or exercises.

What Are the Other Books in this Series? Which One Should I Read Next?

Currently there are five other books in the series.

> Top 50 grammar mistakes - *how to avoid them*
> Wordsearches - *widen your vocabulary in English*
> Test your personality - *quizzes that are fun and improve your English*
> Word games, riddles and logic tests - *boost your English and have fun*
> Jokes - *have a laugh and improve your English*

Apart from the grammar book, the other four books are designed to be dipped into rather than being read from the first page to the last. 'Dipped into' means that you can pick up the book and read any page you like, and for as long as you like.

You are likely to have more fun with the books if you read two or three at the same time. So rather than spending the next month concentrating exclusively on vocabulary or grammar, you might find it more fun and stimulating to read a few jokes from the Jokes book, and do a few word searches and quizzes.

Teachers Introduction

Which Vocabulary Mistakes Were Chosen and Why?

How do you choose the top vocabulary mistakes when you're writing for an international audience?

My solution was to find books of typical mistakes made by speakers of some of the most important languages in the world: Chinese, French, Italian, German, Japanese, Portuguese, Russian and Spanish. I also had access to mistakes made by Czechs, Poles, and Romanians. I then looked to see what mistakes in English were common to the majority of these languages. You can find a list of these books in the next subsection.

I was somewhat hampered by the fact that one of the two books I had on Chinese mistakes and the only book I could find on Japanese mistakes were in the native languages, and I was thus only able to read the sentences in English. I am also influenced by the fact that I live and teach in Italy, and therefore have a natural tendency towards noticing and recording mistakes by speakers of Latinate languages - French, Portuguese, Romanian and Spanish. Thus I would say that my book suffers from a bias of containing more 'European' mistakes than any other.

What was interesting was the sheer number of mistakes that all these disparate languages share. For example, the mistake *I am in London since two weeks* is a mistake that would be made by almost any non-native English speaker in the world. Likewise, the false friend *actually* which derives from Latin and is similar in meaning to the Latin, is only used in the meaning of *in reality* in English, but not in Italian (and other Latinate languages), but not in German, Polish, Russian etc. either.

So essentially what you have is a somewhat subjective choice of words that are frequently confused by speakers of many languages. However, it would be fair to say that another author might have come up with quite a different set of words.

One thing that makes my book different from most of the others, is that it groups words together. Nearly all the others, have one word headings such as *bring*, whereas this book lists *bring* along with the words it is frequently confused with: *take, carry, fetch* etc.

In any case, all the mistakes listed in this book and in its companion book on Grammar mistakes are extremely common. If your students manage to master the differences between the various words and constructions, then their English will improve massively - much more so than trying to learn all English vocabulary or all grammar items.

How Should I Use this Book?

The exercises in this book can be used to test student's proficiency with particular sets of words with similar meanings.

They are best used after a specific mistake has been made by a student. For example, if a student misuses *say* and *tell*, and you believe that this is a recurrent mistake or is likely to be made by others in the class, then you can:

- write the mistake on the whiteboard
- refer students to the explanation of the differences - example sentences are highlighted in a grey background in each section, and are followed by guidelines to usage
- check your students' understanding - in a monolingual class, you can give them a few examples in their own language for them to translate. For example, most languages only have one word that translates both *say* and *tell*. Or there might also be confusion between *say* and *speak*
- give them the exercise

A few lessons later you can then revise the point, by giving students the relevant exercise from the exercise contained in Part II Revision Tests.

Where Can I Find More Grammar Explanations and Tests?

Top 50 grammar mistakes is aimed at students studying general English. I have also written a series of books on academic English.

If you want more detailed grammar explanations, then you can find them in this book:

English for Research: Grammar, Usage and Style https://link.springer.com/book/10.1007/978-1-4614-1593-0

If you would like to do extra grammar exercises and see examples of English sentences in a more technical context, then you can use this book:

English for Academic Research: Vocabulary Exercises https://link.springer.com/book/10.1007/978-1-4614-1593-0

The companion to *Top 50 vocabulary mistakes*, which is entitled *Top 50 Grammar Mistakes*, also contains many exercises that you might find useful. You can find the index to Grammar book on page 169.

By using all these books in combination, you should be able to create lessons that cater to all levels and needs of students.

In the appendix, you can find the index to the *Grammar Exercises* and the Table of Contents of the *Vocabulary Exercises* book. This will help you to find additional grammar explanations or exercises.

Books Consulted

I consulted hardback copies of the following books, which are all part of my personal library.

Angielski bez błędów, George Sliwa, Wydawnictwo Literackie, 2001

Common English Errors in Hong Kong, David Bunton, Longman 1989

Diccionario de dudas, A & J Merino, Editorial Paraninfo, 1990

Engleza fara greseli / L'anglais sans fautes, Lionel Dahan, Larousse, 1995

English or Czenglish? Don Sparling, Statni pedagogicke nakladatelstvi, 1989

Il tuo inglese senza errori, Adrian Wallwork, De Agostini

Longman Dictionary of Common Errors, Heaton & Turton, Longman, 1987

Portuglish, Stephen Fordham, Platano Editora, 1997

Stop Making Mistakes, Robert Kleinschroth, Rewohlt Taschenbuch Verlag, 2003

The Mistakes Clinic for German-speaking Learners of English, Geoff Parkes, Englang Books, 2001

Trudnosti anglijskogo slovoupotreblenia. (English Trouble Words for Russian Speakers). S.S. Khidekel, M.R. Kaul, and R.S. Ginsburg, Moscow: AST, Astrel', 2002

I was unable to find full details of these two books as they are written totally in Chinese and Japanese, respectively:

Contemporary English - a book of typical mistakes made by Chinese speakers, 1998

Typical mistakes made by Japanese, Tim Young, 2005

Acknowledgements

I would like to thank above all my students from the last 25 years who provided the vast majority of the mistakes collected in this book and the companion volume on Grammar.

I would also like to thank those students and readers who gave or sent me copies of books of typical mistakes made in their English. Thanks to Mike Seymour for the books on mistakes made by Germans.

Thank you Anna Southern for trawling through this book to find my mistakes!

Author's Request to Teachers
It would be great if you could contribute to future editions. Please send me examples or explanations that you would like me to include. Please be as specific as possible, provide clear examples, and highlight to me why you think the 'mistake' should be included.

Please also let me know if you find any typos or explanations and keys to exercises that you don't agree with.

Finally, feel free to contact me (adrian.wallwork@gmail.com) if you have ideas for other books that could be part of this Easy English series.

Please also check out our self published books at: **sefl.co**.uk

About the Author

Since 1984 I have been teaching English as a foreign language - from General English to Business English to Scientific English. I have taught students of all nationalities, and this book is based primarily on the typical mistakes that these students make. I am the author of over 30 textbooks for Springer Science+Business Media, Cambridge University Press, Oxford University Press, the BBC, and many other publishers.

Part I
Top 50 Vocabulary Mistakes

Chapter 1
According to

According to me, this will never work.

In my opinion / I think this will never work.

According to his opinion, it was my fault.

In his opinion / view ... He **thinks / believes / reckons** that it was ...

You must according to the doctor's advice.

You must **follow** the doctor's advice.

According to the accident, she arrived late for the party.

As a result of / Owing to / Because of ...

According to all these reasons, we decided to abandon the project.

For all these reasons, we ...

According to my husband, they are building a new supermarket here.

According to Einstein, time is an illusion.

The meeting all went **according to** schedule.

According to the table set out in Annex IV of the proposal.

As a result of / Owing to / Because of her illness she had to stop work.

Guidelines

- **according to** a person but not *me*
- **according to** a source (document, report, institute, figure)
- **as a result of / owing to / because of** - as a consequence of
- **for a reason** - gives an explanation for something

Some sentences are correct others are not: Correct the incorrect sentences

1. Proposals are sorted **according to** their price, quantity and time priority.
2. They were used **according to** the manufacturer's operating manual.
3. **According to** me they should all leave now.
4. She was forced to give up her job **according to** her poor health.
5. You should **according to** your teacher's wishes.
6. **According** to the power cut, the school had to be closed.
7. **According to** our estimates about 30,000 people will be coming to the concert.
8. She always arrived to work on time, **according to** her colleagues.
9. **According to** Mayan prophecies a serpent rope will appear in the center of the Milky Way.
10. Alcohol was to blame for the outbreak of violence, **according to** a source at the police station.
11. He's completely mad **according to** me.
12. **According to** a newspaper report, she fell ill with a stomach problem during her tour.
13. He is a strong believer in equality between men and women, **according** to those that have worked with him.
14. **According to** these reasons, they had to leave early.
15. Children should be punished **according to** her opinion.

All correct except:

3) In my opinion / I think they should all leave now.
4) She was forced to give up her job due to / as a result of her poor health.
5) You should follow your teacher's wishes.
6) Due to / As a result of / Because of the power cut, the school had to be closed.
11) He's completely mad in my view / in my opinion. // I think he is ...
14) For these reasons ...
15) Children should be punished in her opinion. // She thinks ...

Chapter 2
Actual, Actually

The information on the website is not actual.

The information on the website is not **up to date / current**.

This is a very actual question in US politics.

This is a very **topical** question.

So what do you do? I am a trained account but actually I am between jobs.

But I am between jobs **at the moment / currently**.

I was born in Morocco but I actually live in Peru.

But **now** I live in Peru.

I moved the now apartment last month.

I move to **my current** apartment last month.

> The **actual** results are totally different from those predicted.
>
> My textbook says that 100,000 people died in the war, but the **actual** figure was much higher.
>
> The events that she recounted and the **actual** events as they really happened are very different.
>
> You live in Peru, don't you? **Actually**, I live in Colombia which is just to the north.
>
> Did you have fun at the party? Well **actually** it was rather boring.

Guidelines

- **actual** = true, real
- **actually** = in reality, to tell the truth
- **up to date** = the most recent
- **topical** = of interest at the moment
- **current(ly)** = at the moment
- **nowadays** = contrasts with how things were in the past

Choose the correct form

1. This problem is very **actual / current / topical** at the moment
2. The **actual / current / topical** financial crisis has focused public attention on the rapid growth of homelessness. It is difficult to establish the **actual / current / topical** numbers of homeless people, as not all homeless people register as being homeless.
3. The **actual / current / topical** words she used were taken as evidence.
4. Young people are interested in **actual / current / topical** problems such as climate change.
5. Several thousand people have been reported as dying, but the **actual / current / topical** number is still not known.
6. Hundreds of people are dying, and the **actual / current / topical** number of dead stands at 565.
7. Are you living with a colleague? **Actually / Currently** I am living with my boss!
8. I am **actually / currently** living with a work colleague, but next week I am moving into my own flat.
9. Did you enjoy the film? **Actually / Currently** I thought it was a bit boring.
10. Grime music is **actually / currently** enjoying a comeback in many parts of the UK.
11. **Nowadays / Currently / Actually** the use of wireless connections is undergoing a radical change.
12. This raises the issue of whether such treatments **nowadays / currently / actually** influence the outcome of the illness or not.
13. This product was once very expensive to manufacture. However **nowadays / currently / actually** it is much cheaper, **nowadays / currently / actually** it hardly costs anything at all.
14. Are some supposedly poor schools **nowadays / currently / actually** rich in other ways?
15. There is no evidence that categorically shows that cannabis **nowadays / currently / actually** stunts the growth of fetuses.

1 topical 2 current, actual 3 actual 4 current, topical 5 actual 6 current 7 actually 8 currently 9 actually 10 currently 11 currently 12 actually 13 nowadays, actually 14 actually 15 actually

Chapter 3
Advice, Advise

Please can you give me one advice?

Please can you give me **some advice.**

They gave me many good advices.

They gave me **a lot of good advice.**

I advice you to visit the museum.

I **advise** you to visit the museum.

I advise to see the doctor.

I **advise you** to see.

> Let me give you a couple of **pieces of advice**.
>
> She **advised** me to go immediately.
>
> She **advised** that I should go immediately.
>
> She **advised** going immediately.
>
> A window **warns** the user if the computer is about to explode.
>
> The manager has **advised** the work force that they will all be sacked/fired.

Guidelines

- **advice** = uncountable; you cannot say *one advice, two advices*
- **advise** = to present a recommended/sensible course of action
- **advise** = you advise someone to do something (advise + person + infinitive)
- **advise** = to inform (very formal)
- **warn** = advise someone about some possible danger

Some sentences are correct, others are not. Correct the incorrect sentences

1. I followed your **advice** and took the night off.
2. I **adviced** him to call the police.
3. I asked her for some **advise**.
4. They gave us many useful **advices**.
5. She asked an **advice** to her accountant.
6. But honestly, your **advice** was great.
7. Surprisingly, my mother was giving good **advices**.
8. She's here to **advise** and to help.
9. I must **advise** you this interview is being recorded.
10. My lawyer should be here to **advise** me.

All correct except:

2) I advised him
3) for some advice
4) a lot of useful advice/much useful advice
5) She asked her accountant for some advice.
7) good advice

Chapter 4
Agree

Are you agree with me? Yes, I am agree.

Do you agree with me? Yes, I **agree**.

I am not agree with you.

I **don't agree** with you.

We were both agreed that it was the right thing to do.

We both **agreed** that ...

I don't agree people who vote right wing.

I don't **agree with** people who vote right wing.

Few people agreed helping us.

Few people **agreed to** help us.

Do you agree what he said?

Do you **agree with** what he said?

Do you agree with my opinion?

Do you **share my** opinion? Do you **agree with me?**

> I **agree** with you.
>
> **Do you agree** with me?
>
> No, I **don't agree** with you.
>
> We **agreed** to meet later in the week.
>
> I **agreed** with her / I shared her opinion.

Guidelines

- **to agree** = regular verb, no *be / is / was* etc is required
- **to agree + with**
- **to agree to do something** (agree + infinitive)

Some sentences are correct, others are not. Correct the incorrect sentences

1. My husband is never **agree** with me about anything.
2. Do you **agree** with her opinion?
3. I am not **agree** with you that everyone is equal.
4. Were you **agree** with what they said?
5. I didn't **agree** that it was the right thing to do.
6. We were **agreed** to go.
7. Most people didn't not **agree** contributing money to the cause.
8. Do you **agree** that we need to talk about it?
9. Did they **agree** what she said?
10. I hadn't **agreed** to go but in the end they had forced me.

All correct except:

1) My husband never agrees with me about anything.
2) Do you agree with her?
3) I do not agree with you that everyone is equal.
4) Did you agree with what they said?
6) We (had) agreed to go.
7) Most people didn't not agree with contributing / agree to contribute money to the cause.
9) Did they agree with what she said?

Chapter 5
Among, Between, Of, From

Many people can't distinguish among red and green.

Many people can't distinguish **between** red and green.

Unemployment between graduates is estimated at higher than 40%.

Unemployment **among** graduates is estimated at higher than 40%.

Luxembourg lies among Belgium, Germany and France.

Luxembourg lies **between** Belgium, Germany and France.

Tomorrow's temperature will vary between 20 to 25 degrees.

Tomorrow's temperature will vary **between** 20 **and** 25 degrees. / **from** 20 **to** 25 degrees.

Next week your uncle will be among us.

Next week your uncle will be **here with** us.

Illiteracy is commonest under rural women.

Illiteracy is commonest **among** rural women.

> He was standing **between** Paul and Joseph.
>
> She was standing **among** a crowd of hooligans.
>
> **Between** you and me, I think she's mad.
>
> They divided the cake **between / among(st)** them.
>
> We've got various options to choose **from**.
>
> **Of** the three books, my favorite is this one.
>
> Inflation is likely to vary **between** 10% **and** 13%.
>
> **Among** the first to arrive was my sister.

Guidelines

- **between** = two different items or groups of distinct items
- **among** = a number of indistinct different items
- **of** = before an indeterminate number of the same item
- **from** = after a verb when making a selection (*choose from, pick from, select from*)
- **from ... to / and** = for a range

Choose the correct form

1. **Among / Between / From / Of** the factors to be considered are X, Y and Z.
2. Profits are divided **among / between / of** the workers and the share-holders.
3. **Among / Between / From / Of** the methods we have tried so far, this is certainly the best.
4. Our house is **among / between / from / of / with** the woods, the river and the village.
5. **Among / Between / From / Of** the ten candidates, there was not even one that satisfied our needs.
6. Do we have to choose **among / between / from / of** these questions?
7. I thought Cambridge was the most interesting **among / between / from / of** the cities I went to.
8. His house is hidden **among / between / from / of** the trees.
9. I felt that I was **among / between / from / of** friends.
10. Many species have died out, **among / between / from / of** them X, Y and Z are the most well known.
11. Tibet is situated **among / between / of** India, Pakistan and China.
12. We had to choose **among / between / of** several candidates.

1) of 2) between 3) of 4) between 5) of 6) from 7) of 8) among 9) among 10) of 11) between 12) between

Chapter 6
Appreciate

I would appreciate if you could make less noise.
I would **appreciate it** if you could make less noise.
The attendees appreciated the talk by applauding.
The attendees **applauded** when the speaker finished.
Their efforts should be appreciated in some way.
Their efforts should be **rewarded** in some way.
Pink Floyd are appreciated by some of my friends.
Some of my friends **like** Pink Floyd.

> I would **appreciate it** if you could send me the file as an attachment.
>
> I **appreciate** that you don't have much time.
>
> Thank you so much, I really **appreciate** what you did for me.
>
> I don't feel **appreciated**. It seems to me that other people do not value what I do.

Guidelines

- **appreciate** = to express an understanding that something is valuable / helpful
- **appreciate** the fact that someone does something for you
- **would appreciate** + *it* + person + *would / could*
- **like** = to find music / food / art good
- **reward** = officially recognize with some kind of payment, honor

Some sentences are correct, others are not. Correct the incorrect sentences

1. I would appreciate if you could come a little early.
2. I really appreciate what she does for me.
3. Your telling people exactly what you think may be appreciated by some people on some particular occasions.
4. It is very important to me that others appreciate my achievements.
5. Would you do me a huge favor and lend me your bike - I'd really appreciate it.
6. This is clearly not the best approach but I hope you will appreciate the reasons for me choosing this line of action.
7. I appreciate the food at this restaurant.
8. I appreciate the effort you have made.
9. The audience appreciated the movie by getting up and clapping at the end.
10. This kind of behavior is not appreciated here.
11. I appreciate a man who speaks his mind.
12. I think I'd appreciate a day by myself.
13. I would really appreciate a cup of coffee.
14. I would appreciate a response within the next 24 hours.
15. I appreciate your enthusiasm, but I am not sure it is really merited.

All correct apart from:

1) I would appreciate if it you could come a little early.
7) I (really) like the food at this restaurant.
9) At the end movie the audience got up and clapped.
10) This kind of behavior is not tolerated here. We do not like this kind ...
11) I like a man who speaks his mind.
12) I think I'd like a day by myself.
13) *Alternative*: I would really like a cup of coffee.

Chapter 7
As, Like

He's acting like the manager until the real boss comes back.
He's acting **as** the manager until the real boss comes back.
She started to cry as a baby.
She started to cry **like** a baby.
This Monday, as all Mondays, there will be a meeting.
This Monday, **like** all Mondays, there will be a meeting.
She plays as you.
She plays **like** you / **as well as** you do.
It looks as they won't be coming.
It looks **as if** they won't be coming.
They looked as they were disappointed.
They looked **as if** they were disappointed.
I prefer red fruits as strawberries and raspberries.
I prefer red fruits **such as** strawberries and raspberries.

> Luigi is acting **as** manager while Carlo is away. (Luigi becomes a temporary manager).
>
> Luigi acts **like** a manager (he dresses smart, gives people orders etc) – but he is not a manager.
>
> He eats **like** a pig.
>
> I can't speak English **as** well **as** you can.
>
> They look **as if** they have been under the sun too long.
>
> Several countries, **such as** Chile, Peru and Bolivia, have suffered from this problem.

Guidelines

- **as** - in the role of
- **like** - similar to but not the real thing; in the same way as
- **the same + as**
- **(not) as ... as** - to make comparisons highlighting that two things are (not) equal
- **such as** - to give examples
- **look, seem, sound** + *as if* + verb

Choose the correct form

1. The film was terrible, it wasn't anything **as / like** I imagined.
2. The second house has the same number of rooms **as / like** the first house.
3. **As / Like** can be seen in the table, the values are considerably lower this time.
4. **As / Like** a prototype it worked well, but not in its final version.
5. It behaves **as / like** the other one.
6. Teacher to student: I am telling you this **as / like** your friend not **as / like** your teacher.
7. It can be used **as / like** an alternative.
8. I don't earn as much money **as / like** I used to but I work a lot less.
9. We used a piece of wood **as / like** a lever.
10. It looks **as / like** if it is going to rain.
11. We have many different products such **as / like** phones, radios, PCs.
12. His mother, **like / as** his father, comes from Hong Kong.

1) like 2) as 3) as 4) as 5) like 6) as, as 7) as 8) as 9) as 10) as 11) as 12) like

Chapter 8
Available, Comfortable, Convenient

What time are you convenient?

What time are you **available**? / What time **is convenient for you**?

She is a very available person.

She is a very **helpful** person. / She is always **willing to help**.

It's very comfortable living in the center of town.

It's very **convenient** living in the center of town.

It is more comfortable to download them.

It is **simpler / easier** just to download them.

It is not convenient to do X, it is better to do Y.

It is not **a good idea** to do X, it is better to do Y.

This chair is not very comfort.

This chair is not very **comfortable.**

I hope he takes it comfortable.

I hope he takes **his time**.

Please be available at six to leave the hotel.

Please be **ready / prepared** at six to leave the hotel.

> Would you be **available** after 6 pm? / Would after 6 pm be **convenient** for you / 6 pm **suit** you?
>
> I am **available** at any time to suit you.
>
> Where I park my car is not very **convenient** (i.e. it is not close to where I live).
>
> The train only goes once an hour, so it is not very **convenient**.
>
> There are trains every 10 minutes, which is really **convenient**.
>
> This sofa is very **comfortable**.
>
> I bought this sofa at a **very good / cheap price**.
>
> They **took their time** in preparing the food.

Guidelines

- **available** - free from commitments
- **helpful, approachable** - willing to help, easy to talk to
- **convenient** - at a good time, in a good location
- **a good idea** - the best approach
- **comfortable** - easy fitting / relaxing clothes or furniture
- **take one's time** - not rush or hurry

Choose the correct form

1. It's very **convenient / available / comfortable** living in the center of the city.
2. This is a very **convenient / good idea / comfortable** apartment, we have everything we need.
3. There is a supermarket round the corner from my house which is really **convenient / available / comfortable** if I need milk and bread.
4. It is not **a good idea / convenient** to do more than one test at a time.
5. Let me know what time it would be **convenient / available / comfortable** for you to meet.
6. Let me know when you are **convenient / available / comfortable** to meet.
7. Organizing a conference on this topic would be a **convenient / available / comfortable** way of getting everyone interested together in one room.
8. Holding the conference on a pacific island would be fun but not very **convenient / good idea / comfortable** for most attendees.
9. The beds in the hotel were particularly **convenient / available / comfortable**.
10. I was very **convenient / available / comfortable** lying in your bed.
11. I wonder if now would be **convenient / available / comfortable**.

12. Try adjusting the position, you might be more **convenient / available / comfortable**.
13. Sorry it's really not **convenient / available / comfortable** for me to talk right now.
14. She's been here a week now: smart, **available / helpful / convenient** and very thorough.
15. It's not **available / comfortable / helpful** to the general public yet.

1) convenient 2) comfortable 3) convenient 4) a good idea 5) convenient 6) available 7) convenient 8) convenient 9) comfortable 10) comfortable 11) convenient 12) comfortable 13) convenient 14) helpful 15) available

Chapter 9
Beautiful, Good, Fine, Nice

She gets a beautiful salary.

She gets a **good** salary.

It is a beautiful film - excellent plot, lots of action and a great soundtrack.

It is a **good / great** film - excellent plot, lots of action and a great soundtrack.

He is a beautiful man.

He is a **good looking** man.

The most beautiful thing about this job is that I only have to work three days a week.

The **best thing** about that job is that I only have to work three days a week.

We had beautiful weather on our short holidays, just a bit of rain and few cloudy days.

We had **good** weather / The weather was **fine** ...

How are you? Not very fine.

How are you? Not very **good / well**.

She studies the beautiful arts.

She studies the **fine** arts.

> She is the most **beautiful** woman in the world.
>
> It was a **beautiful** film - the photography was amazing.
>
> It was a **good / great** film - lots of exciting moments.
>
> It was a **nice** film - nothing amazing, but I enjoyed it.
>
> What was the weather like? **Beautiful** (lots of sunny days), **nice / good** (not amazing but still good), **fine** (not bad, but not particularly good).

Guidelines

- **beautiful** - aesthetically pleasing
- **good** - showing high quality
- **nice** - quite good; friendly
- **fine** - perfectly acceptable
- **great** (see Chapter 11) - really good, really high quality, strong expression of approval

Choose the correct word

1. What is the weather like? It is not very **beautiful / fine / good / nice**.
2. What is the book like? It is very **beautiful / fine / good / nice**.
3. Italy is a very **beautiful / fine / good / nice** place.
4. It'd be really **beautiful / fine / good / nice** to talk to somebody about it.
5. It's so **beautiful / fine / good / nice** to see you away from that computer.
6. It's so **beautiful / fine / good / nice** to hear, you guys.
7. She's almost, in my opinion, too **beautiful / fine / good / nice** for this world.
8. It would be **beautiful / fine / good / nice** to travel more, I suppose.
9. It will be **beautiful / fine / good / nice** after we have finished the exams.
10. Your hair has a really **beautiful / fine / good / nice** energy.
11. Your father had a weakness for **beautiful / fine / good / nice** strong women.

The key lists the most likely choices:

1) good, nice 2) good 3) beautiful 4) good, nice 5) nice 6) good, nice 7) beautiful, good, nice 8) nice, good 9) good, nice 10) beautiful 11) beautiful

Chapter 10
Because, Why

Because her terrible English, no one understood a word she said.

Because her English is terrible, no one understood a word she said.

Because she was too young, so she couldn't watch the movies.

Because she was too young, **she** couldn't watch the movies.

I don't see why is this man so angry.

I don't see w**hy this man is** so angry.

She wants to make a contribution to the community therefore she does community service.

She wants to make a contribution to the community **that's why** she does community service.

Why haven't you finished the homework? It is because I didn't have time.

Why haven't you finished the homework? **Because** I didn't have time.

Why not to do it now?

Why not do it now?

Why to go there when you could stay here?

Why go there when you could stay here?

They asked me the reason for which I had done it.

They asked me **why** I had done it.

I did not study much. Because of it I failed the exam.

I did not study much **so** I failed the exam./ I failed the exam **because** I did not study much.

> **Why** did you tell him? I told him **because** I thought he should know the truth.
>
> This is **why** I don't tell you things, **because** you always end up crying.
>
> Student: I can't understand this equation. Math teacher: **That's because** you are not a mathematician like me.
>
> Student: I had a horrible math teacher at school. He used to hit me when I made a mistake. Other person: Well **that is** probably **why** you don't like math.

Guidelines
- **because** - for the reason that
- **why** - in questions to ask a reason
- **that's why** - refers to the cause; given as an explanation for an already known fact / event
- **that's because** - refers to the consequence

Some sentences are correct, others are not. Correct the incorrect sentences

1. Because her husband had died, so she had to support her family.
2. Road safety is a fundamental issue why it helps to protect lives. That is why we have traffic lights and ...
3. Our aim was to find out because working out teachers' timetables is such a time-consuming process.
4. The students failed the exam. This was why they hadn't studied and this is also why they will have to retake it.
5. See, this is why we're perfect together - we understand each other so well.
6. I failed the exam. Because of it I cannot go to college.
7. We went to Australia via Bangkok because it cost less, and that's because we took 32 hours to get there rather than 22.
8. There are three reasons why this is important.
9. But this is exactly why I am here - to help you.
10. Because you came late?

1. Because her husband had died, **she** had to support her family.
2. Road safety is a fundamental issue **because** it helps to protect lives. That is why we ...
3. Our aim was to find out **why** working out teachers' timetables is ...
4. This was **because** they hadn't studied and this is also why they will have to retake it.

5. OK
6. I failed the exam **so** I cannot go to college. **Because** I failed the exam I cannot go to college.
7. We went to Australia via Bangkok because it cost less and that's **why** we took ...
8. OK
9. OK
10. **Why did you come** late?

Chapter 11
Big, Great, Large

I paid a big amount for the tickets.

I paid a **large** amount for the tickets.

Your company is great enough to be considered a middle-sized company.

Your company is **large** enough to be considered a middle-sized company.

Quite a big number of people voted for Trump.

Quite a **large** number of people voted for Trump.

He has a big disease.

He has a **serious** disease.

The meeting was attended by a large number of audience.

The meeting was attended by a **large audience**.

I have a big hunger.

I **am very hungry**.

I hope you don't think my article is too big.

I hope you don't think my article is too **long**.

> They live in a **big** house.
>
> Seattle is a **big / large** city with around 700,000 inhabitants.
>
> He's my **big** brother, four years old than me.
>
> There was a **large** quantity of heroine in her suitcase.
>
> He is a **large** man - over two meters tall and weighing around 120 kg.
>
> It was a truly **great** discovery.
>
> Berlin is a **great** city - there is so much to do.
>
> Mahatma Gandhi was a **great** man.
>
> She is a **great** English teacher - very friendly and very knowledgeable.

Guidelines

- **big / large** - physical size, + reference to older family members
- **large** + amount, number, quantity
- **great** - character, personality, of big impact

Insert *big*, *large*, *great*, *serious* or *long* into the spaces.

1. And at _____ personal sacrifice, to myself ...
2. Have a seat, watch the _____ screen.
3. I wrote this _____ essay but the teacher wasn't pleased with it.
4. It is a _____ illness.
5. It would be a _____ step up for me.
6. There's _____ gig on Wednesday - are you going?
7. That must've created _____ unhappiness for you.
8. My annoying _____ sister is coming for lunch.
9. They must have had a pretty _____ family.
10. Two _____ pepperoni pizzas, please.
11. You made a _____ mistake.
12. Your lies have caused me a _____ deal of embarrassment.

1. And at **great** personal sacrifice, to myself...
2. Have a seat, **watch** the big screen.
3. I wrote this **long** essay but the teacher wasn't pleased with it.
4. It is a **serious** illness.
5. It would be a **big** step up for me.
6. There's **big** gig on Wednesday - are you going?
7. That must have created **great** unhappiness for you.
8. My annoying **big** sister is coming for lunch.
9. They must have had a pretty **big** family.
10. Two **large** pepperoni pizzas, please.
11. You made a **big** mistake.
12. Your lies have caused me a **great** deal of embarrassment.

Chapter 12
Borrow, Lend, Loan

Can I lend your pen a minute please?

Can I **borrow** your pen a minute please?

Can you borrow me your car?

Can you **lend** me your car?

I borrowed my car to a friend.

I **lent** my car to a friend.

My friend has borrowed me her bike.

My friend has **lent** me her bike.

The bank borrowed us the money.

The bank **loaned** us the money.

Can I borrow your bathroom?

Can I **use** your bathroom?

Can I **borrow** this book (from you)?

Could you **lend** this book to me? Could you **lend** me this book?

She **lent** me her bike.

I **borrowed** her bike (from her).

Libraries **loan** books, banks **loan** people money.

Guidelines

- **borrow** - something you take from the owner for temporary use
- **borrow money** - from a friend, bank etc
- **lend** - an owner gives you something on a temporary basis
- **lend a hand / support** - help
- **loan** - a bank or person loans money to someone else

Choose the correct form

1. He is **borrowing / loaning / lending** us his private jet.
2. I shouldn't have **borrowed / loaned / lent** your clothes without asking you - I am very sorry.
3. Besides **borrowing / loaning / lending** books, libraries offer various other services.
4. Can you lend me your cell phone?
5. Fate is hardly **borrowing / loaning / lending** hand.
6. I am not **borrowing / loaning / lending** you any money.
7. I have **borrowed / loaned / lent** a lot of money from my parents.
8. Kelly was **borrowing / loaning / lending** money from your brother for years to pay off his gambling debts.
9. My daughter is **borrowing / loaning / lending** her efforts giving food to the homeless.
10. That is why I am **lending** my wholehearted support to your movement.
11. The money you **borrowed / loaned / lent** me - it wasn't enough.
12. Tom shouldn't have **borrowed / loaned / lent** Mary's car.
13. The bank **borrowed / loaned / lent** us her $100,000 to buy the house.

1. He is **lending** us his private jet.
2. I shouldn't have **borrowed** your clothes without asking you - I am very sorry.
3. Besides **lending** books, libraries offer various other services.
4. Can you **lend** me your cell phone?
5. Fate is hardly **lending** a hand.
6. I am not **lending** you any money.
7. I have **borrowed** a lot of money from my parents.
8. Kelly was **borrowing** money from your brother for years to pay off his gambling debts.
9. My daughter is **lending** her efforts giving food to the homeless.
10. That is why I am **lending** my wholehearted support to your movement.
11. The money you **lent / loaned** me - it wasn't enough.
12. Tom shouldn't have **borrowed** Mary's car.
13. The bank **loaned** us her $100,000 to buy the house.

Chapter 13
Both, Either, Neither

Both of them didn't come to the party.

Neither of them **came** to the party.

Both the two languages are based on Latin.

Both languages are based on Latin.

I don't like both of the novels.

I don't like **either** of the novels.

I don't speak Cantonese and Mandarin.

I don't speak (**either**) Cantonese **or** Mandarin.

I found neither the books on Amazon.

I couldn't find either of the books on Amazon.

In the exam you can neither talk or use a dictionary.

In the exam you **cannot** talk **or** use a dictionary.

Me and my twin sister can both speak English, but we have both problems with Russian.

Me and my twin sister can both speak English, but we **both have** problems with Russian.

Neither she nor I couldn't understand a word.

Neither she nor I **could** understand a word.

We talked to both about the problem.

We talked to **both of them** about the problem.

> **Both** of us are going to the party - we're really looking forward to it.
>
> **Neither** of us are going to the party - we **both** have to study.
>
> After the operation I couldn't eat **or** sleep without difficulty.
>
> After the operation I could **neither** eat **nor / or** sleep without difficulty.
>
> **Neither** parent is coming - **neither** her mother **nor** her father.
>
> **None** of the parents are coming because it's a children-only event.

Guidelines

- **both** = A + B
- **neither ... nor** = not A, not B
- **not ... either** = not A, not B
- **either ... or** = just A or just B but only one of the two

1. This is true **both for / for both** the students (i.e. Jim and Jane) and the professors.
2. This is true **both for / for both** the students (there are 30 in the class) and the professors.
3. This software will **both / either / neither** work with MAC nor with Windows, only on UNIX systems.
4. This software will work with **both / either / neither** MAC or Windows.
5. We had fun **both in / in both** the parks (i.e. Green Park and Hyde Park) we visited and also the museums.
6. We had fun **both in / in both** the parks (we lost count of how many we went to) and the museums.
7. We studied **both / either / neither** English and Spanish. So we don't have any problems translating to and from these two languages.
8. You can study **both / either / neither** English or Spanish, i.e. you only have the option to study one of them.
9. You cannot study **both / either / neither** Russian and Korean, just one of the two.
10. You cannot study **both / either / neither** Russian or Korean, you can only study Chinese.

1. This is true **for both** the students (i.e. Jim and Jane) and the professors.
2. This is true **both for** the students (there are 30 in the class) and the professors.
3. This software will **neither** work with MAC nor with Windows, only on UNIX systems.
4. This software will work with **both** MAC or Windows.
5. We had fun **in both** the parks (i.e. Green Park and Hyde Park) we visited and also ....
6. We had fun **both in** the parks (we lost count of how many we went to) and the museums.
7. We studied **both** English and Spanish. So we ...
8. You can study **either** English or Spanish, i.e. you only have the option to study one of them.
9. You cannot study **both** Russian and Korean, just one of the two.
10. You cannot study **either** Russian or Korean, you can only study Chinese.

Chapter 14
Bring, Take, Carry, Fetch, Get, Lead

An ambulance carried the victim to the hospital.

An ambulance **took** the victim to the hospital.

Shall I bring you home?

Shall I **take** you home?

She brought the baby to bed.

She **put** the baby to bed.

They brought a political debate on TV last night.

They **broadcast / showed** a political debate on TV last night.

We're going to the USA and want to bring medicines with us.

We're going to the USA and want to **take** medicines with us.

Go home and **take** this with you.

Remember to **bring** your laptop to tomorrow's lesson.

I've **taken** the PC to the repair shop.

Thanks for the invitation to the party - shall I **bring** some food?

She's the one who always **carries** the suitcases.

This lift can **carry** up to 10 people.

Can you **[go and] get** my suit from the laundry?

I'm just going to **fetch** the kids from the station.

All roads **lead** to Rome.

Her strange behavior **led** us to believe that she was rather depressed.

Guidelines

- **bring** - is associated with coming here (to where I am)
- **take** - is associated with going there (away from me to somewhere else)
- **carry** - transport in your arms or with your hands; also refers to the physical capacity of some machines
- **get** and **fetch** - go somewhere, collect something and then come back
- **lead** - cause someone or something to go in a particular direction, both in a physical and figurative sense

Some sentences are correct, others are not. Correct the incorrect sentences

1. They **carried** her heavy suitcase for her.
2. Look at what I've **taken** you! Hope you like it.
3. Guest to hosts on phone: What would you like us to **take**?
4. I don't know what to **take** to the dinner at Helmut's tonight.
5. Waiter can you please **bring** me the bill?
6. Teacher: Can you remember to **take** your books to the lesson tomorrow.
7. Everyday I **take** my child to school.
8. I can **bring** the books back to the library for you if you like.
9. I bought a motorbike and last week I went to **take** it from the dealer.
10. All these pressures **brought** to the company shutting down.
11. When I come to the next lesson, I will **bring** it to show you.
12. Could you **take** this book to Kate - she is upstairs.
13. I **take** my child from school at 14.00.
14. Pei Lin, I will be **bringing** a guest, if that's all right.
15. I've got to **take** bread from the baker's - we ordered it this morning.

1) OK 2) brought 3) bring 4) OK 5) OK 6) bring 7) OK 8) take 9) get 10) led 11) OK 12) OK 13) go and get / I fetch 14) OK 15) (go and) get

Chapter 15
Camping, Campsite, Parking, Car Park

On holidays we often go to camping.

On holidays we often **go camping**.

Next weekend we shall have a camping.

Next weekend we are **going camping** / having a **camping trip**.

There are four or five campings along the coast.

There are four or five **campsites** along the coast.

There is a parking near the supermarket.

There is a **car park** near the supermarket.

I couldn't find a parking that's why I am late.

I couldn't find **a parking space / anywhere to park** that's why I am late.

> I like to go **camping** in the summer.
>
> There is a beautiful **campsite** near the beach.
>
> There is a big **car park** outside the city walls.
>
> There is no **parking** for non residents in this area.
>
> Outside my house I have my own private **parking space**.

Guidelines

- **camping** = activity - *go camping, like camping*
- **campsite** = area equipped for tents and caravans
- **parking** = the act of moving a car into a space
- **car park** = place where a lot of cars can park
- **parking space** = place where one car can park

Some sentences are correct others are not. Correct the incorrect sentences.

1. I thought we left the book back at the **campsite**.
2. It's not really a **camping** just an area where you can put up tents.
3. Let's just say he's got a **parking spot** reserved for him downstairs.
4. I couldn't find a **parking** this morning.
5. There are huge **car parks** just out of town but no one uses them.
6. There are three **campings** on the island.
7. I had my wallet have stolen at the **campsite**.
8. I was going to live at the **campsite** to be near her.
9. They turned the field into a **car park**.
10. How would you like your own **parking** closer to the entrance?
11. We had problems **parking** the car.

All correct except:

2) It's not really a **campsite** just an area where you can put up tents.
4) I couldn't find a **parking space / parking spot** this morning.
6) There are three **campsites** on the island.
10) How would you like your own **parking space / parking spot** closer to the entrance?

Chapter 16
Chance, Possibility, Occasion

There is an opportunity that she will come tonight.

There is a **chance** that she will come tonight.

Doing the Erasmus gave me my first occasion to travel abroad.

Doing the Erasmus gave me my first **opportunity** to travel abroad.

Is there any possibility of me borrowing your laptop?

Is there any **chance** of me borrowing your laptop?

This new situation opens up all kinds of chances.

This new situation opens up all kinds of **possibilities / opportunities**.

There is no possibility to control her thoughts.

There is **no way** of controlling / to control her thoughts.

They had the possibility to help us.

They **were able / were in a position** to help us.

We had not other possibilities but to go.

We had no other **choice** but to go.

The more qualified you are the greater the chances to find a job.

The more qualified you are the greater the chances **of finding** a job.

> What are the **chances** of you getting a rise in salary this year?
>
> There is no **chance** of me changing my partner.
>
> Next week I am seeing the boss. It will be a good **opportunity** for me to talk about my career.
>
> What would you do if you won the contract? The **possibilities** are endless.

Guidelines

- **chance** = for future events, unknown things (you have no control)
- **opportunity** = a time when it becomes possible to do something (you have some control)
- **possibility** = something that is possible; option, future choice
- **occasion** = the moment when an event happens

Insert *chance, occasion, opportunity, possibility* **in either the singular or plural form as appropriate**

1. The _____ are just so exciting - there are so many different things we could do.
2. We'd have to win the lottery, and the _____ of that happening are minimal.
3. People kill for _____ like this.
4. Well, what I think we should do is to narrow down the _____ .
5. So the _____ of getting back to sleep again are nil.
6. On that _____ I don't actually remember her saying anything.
7. The _____ of something like that happening again are super-low.
8. She's 52. I've been on the internet and seen that the _____ of her getting pregnant are negligible.
9. We're reviewing the _____ of opening a new branch.
10. Sure. It'll give us a _____ to catch up.
11. Let me give you an _____ to right this wrong.
12. My family also believes in creating _____ for the poor.
13. While were in Australia, we had the _____ to visit our cousins in Sydney.

1. The **possibilities** are just so exciting - there are so many different things we could do.
2. We'd have to win the lottery, and the **chances** of that happening are minimal.
3. People kill for **opportunities** like this.
4. Well, what I think we should do is to narrow down the **possibilities**.
5. So the **chances** of getting back to sleep again are nil.
6. On that **occasion** I don't actually remember her saying anything.
7. The **chances** of something like that happening again are super-low.
8. She's 52, I've been on the internet, the **chances** of her getting pregnant are negligible.
9. We're reviewing the **possibility** of opening a new branch.
10. Sure. It'll give us a **chance** to catch up.
11. Let me give you an **opportunity** to right this wrong.
12. My family also believes in creating **opportunities** for the poor.
13. While were in Australia, we had the **chance / opportunity** to visit our cousins in Sydney.

Chapter 17
Close, Near, Next

I have a flat in the near of the university.

I have a flat **near** the university.

I hope to travel round Asia in the next time / in the coming future.

I hope to travel round Asia in the **near** future.

It's in the near.

It's **nearby**. / It is **not far away**.

There a lot of hills nearby Florence.

There a lot of hills **near** Florence.

We came near to a solution.

We came **close** to a solution.

We went to the near town of Lucca.

We went to the **nearby** town of Lucca.

Where is the next bank?

Where is the **nearest** bank?

I was standing at the bus stop and he came near me.

I was standing at the bus stop and he **came up to** / he **approached** me.

I live very **near / close** to my mother - she lives just down the road.

I am very **close** to my brother - we ring each other every day.

She was standing **next** to me - there was no one in between us.

She was standing **near** to me - just a few people in between.

She was standing **close** to me - she was a bit frightened and cold.

Can you tell me where the **nearest** metro station is?

There are shops at the end of the road and we have a metro station **nearby**.

Turn right at the **next** traffic lights.

I hope to change job in the **near** future.

Guidelines

- **near (+ someone)** - not very far away (from someone); not distant in time
- **next to** - with nothing or no one in between
- **close to** - physically very near someone or something; with a strong relationship
- **nearby** - in the neighborhood, local area

Choose the correct form

1. She is a **close / near** relative to the king.
2. Now I'll be able to be **close / next** to my boyfriend Henry - we'll be at the same university.
3. We live in the house **near / next** door to her.
4. Let's walk to the **closest / nearest** pub.
5. I stood too **close / near** to the fire and burnt my eyebrows.
6. We're running out of gas, let's hope there's a gas station **near / nearby**.
7. Are there any good restaurants **close / near** here?
8. She was standing so **close / next** to me I could feel her breath on my face.
9. I wanted to sit in the seat **close / next** to her, but someone else got their first.
10. I should be getting a promotion in the **near / next** future.
11. I'd like a table **near / close** the back window please.

1. She is a **close** relative to the king.
2. Now I'll be able to be **close** to my boyfriend Henry.
3. We live in the house **next** door to her.
4. Let's walk to the **nearest** pub.
5. I stood too **close** to the fire and burnt my eyebrows.
6. We're running out of gas, let's hope there's a gas station **nearby**.
7. Are there any good restaurants **near** here?
8. She was standing so **close** to me I could feel her breath on my face.
9. I wanted to sit in the seat **next** to her, but someone else got their first.
10. I should be getting a promotion in the **near** future.
11. I'd like a table **near** the back window please.

Chapter 18
Clothes, Dress, Dresses, Get Dressed, Put on, Wear

The boys need some new dresses.

The boys need some new **clothes**.

If they like to wear like that, then who are we to say they shouldn't?

If they like to **dress** like that, then who are we to say they shouldn't?

My three year old child cannot dress by himself.

My three year old child cannot **get dressed** by himself.

Do I have to carry a tie?

Do I have to **wear** a tie / **put** a tie **on**?

I get up and immediately wear my clothes.

I get up and immediately **put my clothes on / get dressed.**

Most of the police force wear guns.

Most of the police force **carry** guns.

She has bought a **dress**, now she needs to buy a jacket to go with it.

She keeps her **clothes**, including her collection of antique wedding **dresses**, in a wardrobe.

I **get dressed** after I have had breakfast.

I always **put on** my right shoe before my left shoe.

I never **wear** the same shoes as the day before.

I usually **dress** very casually.

I usually **wear** very casual **clothes**.

She **wears** her hair long.

I **wear** contact lenses not glasses.

Guidelines

- **clothes** - generic (jacket, T shirt, trousers etc)
- **dress** - typically women only
- **to dress + adverb** - how you wear your clothes (well, formally, casually)
- **to dress someone** - to put clothes on someone
- **to get dressed** - the act of putting your own clothes on
- **to wear** + *clothes, shoes, jewelry, glasses*

Choose the correct form

1. In the morning I **get dressed / wear** very quickly.
2. I usually **dress / wear** scruffy clothes.
3. The boy is **getting dressed / wearing** a nice shirt and trousers.
4. He is **dressed / wearing** very elegantly.
5. I can't get married in this **dress / clothes**.
6. I don't think he can be very rich because his **clothes / dresses** look torn and old.
7. What are you going to **dress / wear** to the party?
8. I get up in the morning, have a shower and then **dress / get dressed**.
9. I notice you're **dressing / wearing** a bracelet today.
10. My dad **dressed / wore** glasses too.
11. He was **dressed / worn** like any other man.
12. I'm the only one in a **dress / cloth**.
13. Peter, your **clothes / dresses** are all over my bedroom floor.
14. He used to help me **get dressed / wear** after my accident - I couldn't dress myself.
15. Would you mind **putting on / wearing** some clothes?
16. He spends most of his money at Armani buying **clothes / dresses**.
17. You need to **dress / wear** formally for work.

1) get dressed 2) wear 3) wearing 4) dressed 5) dress 6) clothes 7) wear 8) get dressed 9) wearing 10) wore 11) dressed 12) dress 13) clothes 14) get dressed 15) putting on 16) clothes 17) dress

Chapter 19
Come, Go

My horrible aunt was staying with us so I didn't want to come back home.

My horrible aunt was staying with us so I didn't want to **go** back home.

I prefer to come back to / return to my house on foot.

I prefer to **go** home on foot.

People coming from Asia are often stereotyped as being good at math.

People **who come** from Asia are often stereotyped as being good at math.

If I don't go now I won't come before it goes dark.

If I don't go now I won't **get back** before it goes dark.

Sorry but we've only just opened and Ms Wang hasn't come back yet.

Sorry but we've only just opened and Ms Wang has not **arrived** yet.

The baby is just learning to go.

The baby is just learning to **walk**.

When does the next bus go?

When **is** the next bus?

When I back to Kobe it was already dark.

When I **got** back to Kobe it was already dark.

> *Imagining that the listener is at the office now.* I **come** to work at 8.30 every morning. I **go** home at around 5.0. What about you, what time do you **get** to work?
>
> *Imagining that the questioner is at home now.* What time are you **coming** home? / What time will you **be** home? Are you **going** to the cinema and then **coming** home?
>
> What time did you **get back** home?
>
> I hope to **go back** to New York next year, which will be the next time I **go** to the USA.
>
> I hope to **come back** and see you the next time I am in your area.

Guidelines

- **come** - move in the direction of the person listening
- **go** - move away from the where the listener is located
- **come back** - return to where listener is
- **go back** - return to a place that is not where the listener is
- **be / get back** - return to a place by a specific time
- **get (to)** - arrive at, go to

Choose the correct form

1. Sorry I am late but I had to **come / go** by bus.
2. I live here but I **come / go** back home every weekend.
3. What time do you generally **come / get** to school?
4. Husband to wife: What time are you **coming / going** home?
5. This time, I'm going to wait for him to **come / go** to me.
6. I shouldn't have **come / gone** to you.
7. I can't **come / go** to Pete's party but I can **come / go** to your party.
8. All right, I have got to **get / come** to work.
9. I don't even want to **go / get** to London - it's too far.
10. He was supposed to **go / get** to New York on Tuesday for business.
11. When I **come / get** home, I'm exhausted.
12. After this, I'm **getting / going** home.
13. Just stay until I **come / go** back from school.
14. If I **come / get** back to you with a million dollars will you marry me?
15. Look, I'll **get / go** back to her, and I will talk to her, and I will find out what she really wants.
16. I am not sure what time I will **be / go** back tonight, so don't wait up for me.

1) come 2) go 3) get 4) coming 5) come 6) come 7) go, come 8) get 9) go 10) go 11) get 12) going 13) come 14) come 15) go 16) be

Chapter 20
Control, Check

They controlled our luggage at the customs.

They **checked / inspected** our luggage at the customs.

Have you controlled what time the train leaves?

Have you **checked / found out** what time the train leaves?

Did you control the translation yet?

Did you **check** the translation yet?

They use a hidden camera to control their children.

They use a hidden camera to **check up on** their children.

I am not sure where she is but I don't control her all the time.

I am not sure where she is but I **don't check up** on her all the time.

We **controlled** the temperature using a thermostat.

We **checked** the temperature and it was fine.

We tested the machines to **check** that they were in working order.

I'll just **check** for you. Yes, she is free for a meeting that morning.

Are you **checking up on** me again? Just leave me alone.

Guidelines

- **control** - actively intervene to ensure that something happens or does not happen
- **check** - verify the status of something, inspect something
- **check up on** - (secretly) find information about someone

Choose the correct form

1. These herbicides are designed to **check / control** the growth of weeds.
2. Parents today seem to be unable to **check / control** their children.
3. Thousands of extra police officers were employed to **check / control** the crowds.
4. I can **check / control** the lighting in my flat directly from my laptop.
5. The ticket inspector is going around **checking / controlling** the tickets.
6. My boss is always **checking up on / controlling** me.
7. It can be difficult to **check / control** a car in icy conditions.
8. The government used terror tactics to **check / control** the people.
9. Our passports were **checked / controlled** at the border.
10. Please can you **check / check up on** the tire pressure.
11. The police were unable to **check / control** the crowd.
12. I'll just **check / control** in my diary to see if I am free.
13. I sometimes find it hard to **check up on / control** my feelings.
14. Don't worry I am not **checking up on / controlling** you, I just want to see how you are getting on.

1) control 2) control 3) control 4) control 5) checking 6) checking up on 7) control 8) control 9) checked 10) check 11) control 12) control 13) check 14) checking up on

Chapter 21
Cook, Cooker, Cooking, Kitchen, Dish, Course, Plate

If you don't like the food don't blame me I am not the cooker.

If you don't like the food don't blame me I am not the **cook**.

I prefer Italian kitchen.

I prefer Italian **cuisine / cooking**.

They serve only traditional plates from the region.

They serve only traditional **dishes** from the region.

What are we having for the main dish / plate?

What are we having for the main **course**?

We have replaced our electric **cooker** with a gas **cooker**.

My husband is an excellent **cook** he's always trying out new recipes.

I like all sorts of **cuisines** but my grandmother's **cooking** is best.

I have cleaned the **kitchen** twice this week already.

This is a typical **dish** from our local area.

There were eight **courses** at the wedding dinner.

They brought in some **plates** of ham and salami.

We have eight guests so we need eight **plates** and eight bowls.

Guidelines

- **cook** - person who cooks (a professional cook is also known as a chef)
- **cooker** - oven
- **cooking** - the way and what a person or a nation cooks (more formal: cuisine)
- **kitchen** - place where you cook
- **dish** - the food served on a plate; *do the dishes - to wash plates, glasses etc*
- **course** - first, second, main
- **plate** - physical object that food is served on

Insert *cook, cooker, cooking, kitchen, cuisine, dish, course* **or** *plate* **into the spaces. In one case you will need to use the plural form**

1. Each episode, they cook a _____ - the worst contestant gets eliminated.
2. I'll still have plenty of room for the main _____ .
3. I'm a pretty terrible _____ , I should warn you.
4. I'm an excellent pianist and a good _____ .
5. I am making a little Mexican _____ called chili.
6. In traditional Japanese _____ there is a progression in how the dishes are served.
7. Our _____ runs on gas.
8. Sit down the first _____ is all set to go.
9. Then there is _____ and bathroom.
10. His favorite _____ was fish pie.
11. This is a disgrace to Italian _____ .
12. The first _____ is a Mexican bean soup.
13. Your mother never liked my _____ .
14. He's in the _____ doing the dirty_____ from last night.
15. The _____ is excellent at that restaurant - he was trained in Paris.

1) dish 2) course 3) cook 4) cook 5) dish 6) cuisine / cooking 7) cooker 8) course 9) kitchen 10) dish 11) cuisine / cooking 12) course 13) cooking 14) kitchen, dishes, 15) cook (chef)

Chapter 22
Do, Make

I mistake. / I did a mistake.

I **made** a mistake.

I am making a course on French cuisine.

I am **doing / taking** a course on French cuisine.

I am making my driving test next week.

I am **doing / taking** my driving test next week. doing

I want to make my PhD in Sweden.

I want to **do** my PhD in Sweden.

I make you a photo.

I'll **take** a photo of you.

Tell me about some of the experiences you made while you were in Peru.

Tell me about some of the experiences you **had** while you were in Peru.

When do you usually make your holidays?

When do you usually **take / have** your holidays?

I'm going to make an eye test.

I'm going to **have** an eye test.

> Did you **do** anything interesting at the weekend?
>
> What are you **doing** with that box?
>
> I **do** everything in this house: I **do** the shopping, I **do** the washing, I **do** the ironing, I **do** the shopping ...
>
> I haven't **done** my homework yet.
>
> These shoes are **made** in Italy.
>
> Can I **make** you a coffee?
>
> She didn't **make** any mistakes.
>
> I'll **make** you a proposal you can't refuse.

Guidelines

- **do** i) anything academic (an exam, homework, a test, some research); ii) anything in the home (the washing, the ironing, the cleaning), iii) generic activities (e.g. *What are you doing?*); iv) favors
- **make** i) with abstract countable nouns - suggestions, choices, proposals, decisions, errors, mistakes; ii) produce something - make cakes, cars, clothes; iii) love, war
- **have** - a shower, a bath, breakfast, lunch, dinner; holidays, breaks
- **take** - photos, a shower, breaks, course

Choose the correct form

1. She **does / makes** a lot of overtime.
2. You're trying to **do / make** the work of two adults.
3. We're trying to **do / make** a weakness into a strength.
4. And I believe she has the skills to **do / make** a fantastic president.
5. We're trying to **do / make** the best for this company, don't you understand?
6. You always **do / make** the unexpected thing.
7. I'm practically **doing / making** the man a favor.
8. The seller was looking to **do / make** a quick sale.
9. I **do / make** all the cleaning in this house. My man **does / makes** nothing.
10. When we are **doing / making** the operation you'll be awake.
11. We have to assume she knew what she was **doing / making**.
12. And I had to **do / make** a choice.
13. But you are **doing / making** a good point.
14. But we've managed to **do / make** a very happy life here.
15. I urge you not to **do / make** a hasty decision.

1) does 2) do 3) make 4) make 5) do 6) do 7) doing 8) make 9) do, does 10) doing 11) doing 12) make 13) making 14) make 15) make

Chapter 23
Early, Soon, On Time, In Time

I hope to see you early - let me know when would suit you.

I hope to see you **soon** - let me know when would suit you.

I hope we've not come too soon - I know it's only 7 o'clock but we were so excited about coming.

I hope we've not come too **early** - I know it's only 7 o'clock but we were so excited about coming.

The buses on this route never arrive in time.

The buses on this route never arrive **on time**.

He came **early** to the lesson i.e. before the lesson was scheduled to start.

I can come at 10.00, or **earlier** if you like.

The contract should be with you **soon** - I can't tell you exactly when, but certainly **in time** for you to be able to sign it before the deadline.

We didn't get to the cinema **on time** - the film had already been going for 60 minutes, but we were obviously **in time** to see the end of the film, which was absolutely amazing.

Guidelines

- **early** - before the allocated / agreed time
- **soon** - at some unspecified time in the near future
- **on time** - at the agreed / specified time
- **in time** - sufficiently early in order to be able to do something

Choose the correct form

1. She left home just **in time / on time** to be at the station at 10.00. In any case, the train didn't actually leave **in time / on time**, it was 20 minutes late.
2. Of the 65 patients given early discharge, more than 75% responded that they felt they had not been sent home too **early / soon**.
3. The onset of this disease can be as **early / soon** as eight years old, and **early / soon** after onset the patient is left feeling permanently weak.
4. I'm sorry it's **early / soon**, but we're leaving **early / soon**, and I needed to talk to you.
5. I was afraid that the present wouldn't arrive **in time / on time** for your birthday.
6. My daughter's not an **early / soon** riser, as you'll **early / soon** discover.
7. She was **in time / on time**, but you are a little late. I don't suppose you have ever arrived **early / soon** in your life.
8. It is too **early / soon** to know what the impact of this initiative will be, so **early / soon** after its inauguration.
9. We hope to be able to send you the document **early / soon / in time**. I would imagine you will receive it some time next week.
10. Our strategy will be adopted **early / soon** - by the end of the year, hopefully, or **early / soon** next year.
11. He didn't get there **in time / on time** to see his son's graduation.
12. They were just **in time / on time** for the last train.
13. The party broke up **early / soon**, but not a minute too **early / soon**.

1) in time, on time 2) soon 3) early, soon 4) early, soon 5) in time 6) early, soon 7) on time, early 8) early, soon 9) soon 10) soon, early 11) in time 12) in time 13) early, soon

Chapter 24
Earn, Gain, Win, Beat, Deserve

She won me easily at tennis.

She **beat** me easily at tennis.

I have deserved the respect of my students.

I have **earned (gained)** the respect of my students.

She has a good job and wins a lot of money.

She has a good job and **earns** a lot of money.

They didn't earn to win.

They didn't **deserve** to win.

At school I learned a lot of knowledge.

At school I **gained** a lot of knowledge.

He **won** the game, in fact he beat me **easily**.

He's **made** a lot of money playing poker.

You need to **gain** some experience before we can promote you.

He's **earned / gained** the respect of his team mates and is now one of the best players we have. He would **deserve** to be nominated player of the year.

You've been working hard - you **deserve /** you **have earned** a break.

Guidelines

- **earn** - receive money for work done; be the worthy receiver of something; respect and reputation
- **make** - money
- **gain** - experience, time, and capital; respect and reputation
- **win** - receive something as a prize; be first in a game
- **beat** - be better than an opponent in a competition (real and figurative)
- **deserve** - merit

Choose the correct form

1. An opposing plan is **earning / gaining** support.
2. And he **deserves / makes** more than you do, over $100,000 per year.
3. It seems the plane is **gaining / winning** altitude.
4. Come on, I want to know who **earned / won** the game.
5. He knows she can't **beat / win** me in court.
6. He's **earning / gaining** confidence, and with good reason.
7. I was tired of singing and not **earning / gaining** anything.
8. Just create an identity, **earn / gain** their trust.
9. Look, you **deserved / won** the bet.
10. My brother **earned / won** the money on the lottery.
11. Tell me how much you **earn / gain** as the director of a store.
12. Scott doesn't **make / gain** enough money to help me out.
13. He loves to **beat / win** me at pool and take my money.
14. She is **earning / gaining** more and more experience.
15. There's no guarantee you'll **beat / win**.
16. We can fool him, **beat / win** him at his own game.
17. What did I do to **earn / deserve** that sarcastic comment?
18. You know who he is and how he **made / gained** his money.

1) gaining 2) makes 3) gaining 4) won 5) beat 6) gaining 7) earning 8) earn / gain 9) won 10) won 11) earn 12) make 13) beat 14) gaining 15) win 16) beat 17) deserve 18) made

Chapter 25
Economic, Economical, Economically, Financial

Our economical situation is bad, neither of us has any money.

Our **financial** situation is bad, neither of us has any money.

The company's economic report is due at the end of the month.

The company's **financial** report is due at the end of the month.

The economical situation in our country is very bad.

The **economic** situation in our country is very bad.

The economical crisis is killing the country.

The **economic / financial** crisis is killing the country.

This car is economic because it does 200 km per liter.

This car is **economical** because it does 200 km per liter.

There should be a period of sustained **economic** growth.

This dishwasher is very **economical** - it has a 25 minute cycle.

Economically / Financially your proposal makes no sense at all.

This project is simply not **financially** viable - it would cost too much money.

My mother's **financial** situation looks really bad, my father left her with a lot of debt.

Guidelines

- **economic** - relating to a country's system of wealth creation and distribution
- **economical** - opposite of wasteful, low consumption
- **economically** - involving careful use of money and resources; relating to economics or finance
- **financial** - regarding someone's or an organization's money situation

Choose the correct form

1. Children are **economically / financially** dependent on their parents.
2. Fuel efficient cars are **economic / economical,** though the extra efficiency comes at a **economical / financial** cost.
3. These are the decisions facing our **economical / financial** institutions.
4. It requires a very **economic / economical** use of interior space.
5. The **economic / financial** performance of several nations in the European Union has been overestimated.
6. The paint should be spread on the surface as **economic / economically** as possible.
7. This is a simple and **economic / economical** method, i.e. it is easy to use and there is no waste involved.
8. This procedure will only be effective and **economical / financial** if productions times are cut considerably.
9. Traders often take unjustified risks in the **economical / financial** markets.

1. Children are **financially** dependent on their parents.
2. Fuel efficient cars are **economical,** though the extra efficiency comes at a **financial** cost.
3. These are the decisions facing our **financial** institutions.
4. It requires a very **economical** use of interior space.
5. The **economic / financial** performance of several nations in the European Union has been overestimated.
6. The paint should be spread on the surface as **economically** as possible.
7. This is a simple and **economical** method, i.e. it is easy to use and there is no waste involved.
8. This procedure will only be effective and **economical** if productions times are cut considerably.
9. Traders often take unjustified risks in the **financial** markets.

Chapter 26
Education, Background, Upbringing, (Good / Bad) Manners, Training

They believe she is a criminal because of her bad education.

They believe she is a criminal because of her bad **upbringing**.

A person's genes and their education are two different things.

A person's genes and their **upbringing** are two different things.

He decided there was no necessity for continuous formation.

He decided there was no necessity for **further education**.

I had a training last week.

I had a **training course** last week.

This formation involves a lot of theoretical knowledge.

This form of **training** involves a lot of theoretical knowledge.

The fact that he has no education is clear - look at the way he behaves on social occasions.

The fact that he has no **manners** is clear - look at the way he behaves on social occasions.

> I had a very Catholic **upbringing** - my parents took me to church every Sunday.
>
> I had a good **education** - my parents sent me to a private school.
>
> His **background** is Latin American, but he acts like he came from Sicily.
>
> My parents taught me **good manners**, especially how to behave at the table.
>
> They expected me to give a presentation, even though I had absolute no **training** in public speaking.

Guidelines

- **education** - what you learn at school
- **upbringing** - what you learn at home
- **background** - cultural or social environment where you were brought up or lived
- **manners** - how you behave socially
- **training** - [uncountable noun] courses on how to do something specific

Choose the correct form

1. Betty's **background / upbringing** - poorest part of town, parents unemployed, shoplifting - explained many of the difficulties she was having in life.
2. Betty had had a very violent **education / upbringing**.
3. Even pigs have more **education / manners** than you just displayed.
4. For that reason, **education / training** must be closely linked with practical work.
5. You could enroll on a **background / training** scheme, a basic literacy program.
6. Although he didn't have a formal **education / training**, he knew his stuff.
7. I think I've evolved beyond my simple rustic **education / upbringing**.
8. I wasn't aware you had any surgical **education / training**.
9. I'd like to focus on **education / manners** and immigration.
10. I'm just saying those girls need to learn some **education / manners**.
11. It is an organization devoted to the **education / manners** of women in the matter of contraception.
12. Social **background / upbringing** must not determine a person's educational opportunities.

1. Betty's **background** - poorest part of town, parents unemployed, shoplifting - explained many of the difficulties she was having in life.
2. Betty had had a very violent **upbringing**.
3. Even pigs have more **manners** than you just displayed.
4. For that reason, **training** must be closely linked with practical work.
5. You could enroll on a **training** scheme, a basic literacy program.
6. Although he didn't have a formal **education**, he knew his stuff.
7. I think I've evolved beyond my simple rustic **upbringing**.
8. I wasn't aware you had any surgical **training**.
9. I'd like to focus on **education** and immigration.
10. I'm just saying those girls need to learn some **manners**.
11. It is an organization devoted to the **education** of women in the matter of contraception.
12. Social **background** must not determine a person's educational opportunities.

Chapter 27
Enjoy, Have A Good Time, Funny, Fun

I enjoyed at the party.

I **enjoyed myself** / I **had a good time** at the party.

We studied very hard but we were enjoying.

We studied very hard but we **enjoyed ourselves**.

I wanted to find a hobby that enjoyed me.

I wanted to find a hobby that I **enjoyed**.

I enjoy to watch football.

I **enjoy** watch**ing** football.

Going to the beach is always funny.

Going to the beach is always **fun**.

It's not fun being around you.

It's **no fun** being around you.

It's not funny being the manager - you have to reprimand people all day.

It's **no fun** being the manager - you have to reprimand people all day.

> Woody Allen made some very **funny** films - they still really make me laugh.
>
> My colleagues are good **fun**. One in particular is very **funny** - he has a wicked sense of humor.
>
> The match was good **fun** to watch.
>
> Working here is not much **fun**.
>
> Did you have **fun** at the party?
>
>> Yes, I **enjoyed myself** a lot. Yes, I **enjoyed** the party a lot.
>>
>> Yes, I **had a good time** at the party. Yes, the party was **fun**.

Guidelines

- **enjoy (doing) something** - find pleasure
- **enjoy yourself** - find pleasure
- **have a good time** - find pleasure, generally on a specific occasion
- **fun** - enjoyable
- **funny** - something that makes you laugh

Choose the correct form, in some cases both may be possible

1. And now they're **enjoying / enjoying themselves** their retirement.
2. Everything's **funnier / more fun** with champagne.
3. **Enjoy / Have fun** at the party!
4. He's very **funny** - he makes us laugh all the time.
5. His lessons are always **fun / funny** - never boring - and we learn a lot.
6. I hope you are **enjoying / having a good time** your work here.
7. I was **enjoying / having fun** some alone time.
8. Make him think his jokes are **fun / funny**.
9. School is **funnier / more fun** than home.
10. She's **having fun / enjoying** and I'm going to do the same.
11. So it looked like you and Alexis were **enjoying yourselves / having a good time**.
12. She told me a couple **fun / funny** stories.
13. It's **no fun / not funny** going to school on a Saturday.

1) are enjoying 2) more fun 3) have fun 4) funny 5) fun 6) enjoying 7) enjoying 8) funny 9) more fun 10) having fun 11) enjoying yourselves, having a good time 12) funny 13) no fun

Chapter 28
Enough, Quite, Pretty, Sufficient

The time is not enough for us to finish this job.

There is not **enough / sufficient** time for us to finish this job.

They didn't have time enough to finish the exercise.

They didn't have **enough / sufficient** time to finish the exercise.

We didn't take enough of food with us.

We didn't take **enough** food with us.

The movie was enough good.

The movie was **quite** good.

One advantage of these airlines is that they are cheap enough.

One advantage of these airlines is that they are **quite** cheap .

This year school is quite harder than last year.

This year school is **quite hard compared** to last year.

I don't have **enough** time to study.

You are good **enough** to pass the exam.

Your English is not good **enough** to do the exam in December.

I am **quite** good at English, but I need to improve my pronunciation.

I am **pretty** good at tennis, in fact I nearly won the championship last year.

I play for **quite** a good team.

Your English is **quite** good - so you may, if you study, pass the exam.

It is not **sufficient / enough** just to study 10 minutes a day.

A **sufficient** amount would be two hours a day.

Your English is **sufficiently** good to pass the exam.

Guidelines

- **enough** + noun
- adjective + **enough** (+ for someone / something + infinitive)
- **quite** + adjective - sufficient or more than sufficient
- **quite** + a / an + adjective + noun
- **pretty** + adjective - much more than sufficient
- **sufficient** (+ noun)
- **sufficiently** (+ adjective)

Some sentences are correct, others are not. Correct the incorrect sentences

1. Although such a system is sufficient popular there is not enough bandwidth to deal with high amounts of traffic.
2. I actually found the truth quite liberating.
3. I am not enough patient to work with children.
4. She left me because I didn't make enough money.
5. She's enough worried about me as it is.
6. That's a quite strong statement.
7. The picture is quite different in the developed countries.
8. The price was increased quite to cover production costs.
9. The results were sufficiently good.
10. You need to get your prices low enough to be competitive.
11. They were not enough old to see the movie - it was an 18 certificate.
12. This house is pretty full as it is.
13. To be honest, I thought it was going enough well.
14. We've had drama sufficient for the night.
15. You can reduce congestion quite substantially.

1) sufficiently popular 2) OK 3) patient enough 4) OK 5) worried enough 6) quite a 7) OK 8) sufficiently 9) OK 10) OK 11) old enough 12) OK 13) pretty / quite 14) enough drama 15) OK

Chapter 29
Even If, Even Though, Although

Even if it was really hot they wore a coat.

Even **though** it was really hot they wore a coat.

Her English is not very good even she has studied it for ten years.

Her English is not very good **even though** she has studied it for ten years.

I prefer red wine to white wine, even if I enjoy white wine too.

I prefer red wine to white wine, **although** I enjoy white wine too.

Although it was raining, but we still went on the picnic.

Although it was raining, **we** still went on the picnic.

> **Even if** you gave me a million dollars I would never lie in court.
>
> **Even though / Although** I am English I do not support the royal family.
>
> **Even if** we had all the time in the world, we would never be able to finish the project.
>
> **Even though / Although** she lives next door, I never see her.

Guidelines

- **even if** - for real situations. It can generally be replaced with *although*
- **although, even though** - for hypothetical situations. Generally followed by the simple past or past perfect

Underline the correct form

1. **Even though / Even if** I studied hard, I still don't think I would pass the exam.
2. **Although / Even if** it was raining heavily, we still went for a walk.
3. **Even though / Even if** you give me all your money, it's not going to make any difference, I don't want to marry you.
4. **Although / even if** role play games intrigue me, I've never really been a big fan of them.
5. **Although / even if** he was extremely rich he lived in a tiny rented apartment.
6. I can still be spiritual **even if / even though** I'm an atheist.
7. **Even though / Even if** I only saw the movie last year, I can't remember anything about it.
8. **Even if / even though** you ask me a million times, I'm not going to tell you.
9. Was the war in Iraq justified, **even if / even though** weapons of mass destruction were not found?
10. When the moon is new, **even if / even though** the weather is clear, the moon will hardly be visible.

1. **Even if** I studied hard, I still don't think I would pass the exam.
2. **Although** it was raining heavily, we still went for a walk.
3. **Even if** you give me all your money, it's not going to make any difference.
4. **Although** role play games intrigue me, I've never really been a big fan of them.
5. **Although** he was extremely rich he lived in a tiny rented apartment.
6. I can still be spiritual **even though** I'm an atheist.
7. **Even though** I only saw the movie last year, I can't remember anything about it.
8. **Even if** you ask me a million times, I'm not going to tell you.
9. Was the war in Iraq justified, **even though** weapons of mass destruction were not found?
10. When the moon is new, **even if** the weather is clear, the moon will hardly be visible.

Chapter 30
Ever, Never, Always

What about this movie? Have you never seen it? It's really great, I think you'd love it.

What about this movie? Have you **ever** seen it? It's really great, I think you'd love it.

He was the worst teacher that I had never had.

He was the worst teacher that I had **ever** had.

He was the worst teacher that I had ever had before.

He was the worst teacher that I had **ever** had.

She has ever been my true love.

She has **always** been my true love.

Taxi drivers always don't know how much they are going to earn.

Taxi drivers **never** know how much they are going to earn.

I am very interested in Japanese but I was never in Japan.

I am very interested in Japanese but I **have never been** to Japan.

Have you **ever** been to Venice? It's a beautiful city.

Have you **never** been to Venice? How come? I thought you were Italian.

Have you **ever** driven at over 200 kilometers per hour?

Have you **never** driven at night before? But that's absurd.

He **always** sits at the front of the class so that he can see the teacher well.

He **never** sits at the front, hoping that the teacher won't ask him any questions.

Guidelines

- **ever** = at some moment in time (**Have you ever ...?** = neutral question)
- **never** = at no moment in time (**Have you never ...?** = I already know the answer and I am surprised)
- **always** = every time, forever, continuously

Choose the correct form

1. Why have you **always / ever / never** told your children that they were adopted?
2. Patients were asked the following questions. 1) Have you **always / ever / never** smoked? 2) Have you ...
3. You must be joking. Have you **always / ever / never** kissed anybody for real?
4. She would **always / ever / never** agree to do that ... not even in a million years.
5. You promised this day would **always / ever / never** come, but here we are.
6. Everybody said that he would **always / ever / never** remarry.
7. Surely she would **always / ever / never** survive two minutes in that job - they would eat her alive.
8. They **always / ever / never** play in public, though there have been many requests.
9. We're **always / ever / never** having problems with him - he behaves atrociously most of the time.
10. Do you think she will **always / ever / never** learn to love me? Maybe it will take a few years.
11. I will **always / ever / never** love you. I feel absolutely nothing for you.
12. Will you **always / ever / never** love me? I mean until the end of time.

1) never 2) ever 3) never 4) never 5) never 6) never 7) never 8) never 9) always 10) ever 11) never 12) always

Chapter 31
Expect, Wait (For)

At the end of her story she expected their reaction.

At the end of her story she **waited for** their reaction.

I'm waiting for an email from them to tell me whether I got the job or not.

I'm **expecting** an email from them to tell me whether I got the job or not.

We took our seats and expected the teacher to come.

We took our seats and **waited for** the teacher to come.

I expected her outside the cinema but she never came.

I **waited for** her outside the cinema but she never came.

I am waiting him at 8 - we have an appointment.

I am **expecting** him at 8 - we have an appointment.

I expect myself that he will be late.

I **expect** that he will be late.

I was waiting that she gave me an explanation.

I was **expecting** her to give me an explanation.

I am waiting that you tell me the answer.

I am waiting **for you to** tell me the answer.

> I'll **expect** you at 10.00 - put it in your diary.
>
> I'll **wait for you** outside the cinema - don't be late.
>
> **Wait** here while I buy the tickets.
>
> I met her at a bus stop while I was **waiting for** the bus to come.
>
> She wasn't what I was **expecting**, much more extrovert than I thought she would be.
>
> I am **expecting** you to study hard for the exam.

Guidelines

- **wait (for)** – stand / sit (possibly wondering when something is going to happen)
- **wait for** someone to do something
- **expect (someone to do something / something to happen)** - know that something is going to happen because you have arranged it or it is inevitable; want, desire, predict

Choose the correct form

1. An employee has a right to **expect / wait** that their salary will improve steadily over the years.
2. Do it quickly, don't **expect / wait**.
3. We will be **expecting / waiting** outside in the car, so don't worry.
4. He probably wasn't **expecting / waiting** to get caught so soon.
5. I know Carina is **expecting / waiting for** you. She's **expecting / waiting for** you in the lounge.
6. I think your teacher is **expecting / waiting for** an apology.
7. I'm not **expecting / waiting for** much trouble.
8. Nobody was **expecting / waiting for** you so soon, Amanda.
9. Since girls tend to initially make faster progress at school, we **expect / wait** that the results of the tests done by the boys will be of a lower level than those done by girls.
10. Surgery took a lot longer than **expected / waited**.
11. We conducted a survey regarding how long a customer can be **expected / waited** to remain on the phone and **expect / wait for** an operator to answer.
12. I have been **expecting / waiting** for months for the commission to get back to me, at this point I am not **expecting / waiting** good news.
13. Why should we **expect / wait for** teachers to teach well when they get paid an average of 6% of what a lawyer earns and yet provide a far more useful service for society in general?
14. Your position will be **expecting / waiting for** you when you return.
15. I **expect / wait for** you to be here on time, so don't be late.
16. I was waiting **that you told / for you to tell / expecting you to** tell me.
17. I will wait **you / for you** here.

1) expect 2) wait 3) waiting 4) expecting 5) expecting, waiting 6) expecting 7) expecting 8) expecting 9) expect 10) expected 11) expected, wait for 12) waiting, expecting 13) expect 14) waiting for 15) expect 16) for you to tell / expecting you to 17) wait for you

Chapter 32
Find, Find Out, Discover, Search, Look For

Can you find what is wrong with my PC, it keeps crashing?

Can you **find out** what is wrong with my PC, it keeps crashing?

I found out some interesting sites on the web.

I **found** some interesting sites on the web.

In the movie he finds out a means to convert iron into gold.

In the movie he **discovers** a means to convert iron into gold.

I have to search my keys every time I leave the house.

I have to **look for** my keys every time I leave the house.

He was looking desperately for something to say.

He was **searching** desperately for something to say.

She hasn't started yet, she's still finding her book.

She hasn't started yet, she's still **looking for** her book.

I am looking for the truth.

I am **searching** for the truth.

I am finding very difficult to learn Chinese.

I am **finding it** very difficult to learn Chinese.

(On the phone) I am looking for Adrian.

(On the phone) **Is** Adrian **there**? // **Could I speak to** Adrian please.

I **found out** that my wife was having an affair - someone saw her kissing another man.

When I came home, I **found** my wife with another man.

Can you **find out** what time the train leaves? And maybe you can **find** tickets on the web.

I'm **looking for** a tie to go with this shirt, but I can't **find** any.

The police **searched** the house but found nothing.

We are **looking for** a house to buy in the country.

They have **discovered** a cure for diabetes.

Guidelines

- **find** - discover or identify something, often by chance
- **find out** - become informed of something
- **look for** - try to find
- **search** - try to find (typically related to the police or the internet)
- **discover** - uncover new information often through formal research

Choose the correct form. More than one form may be possible

1. At the end of the week I **found / found out / discovered** what the problem was.
2. I am **looking for / searching for / finding** my glasses – have you seen them anywhere?
3. I can't **find / find out / search** my glasses, can you help me **find / look for / search for** them?
4. I have **discovered / found / found out** my wallet.
5. I **looked for / searched for** it on Google, but I couldn't **discover / find** it.
6. I **searched / looked for** you everywhere this morning, where were you?
7. I will **find / find out** what's in that briefcase even if it kills me.
8. I am **finding / looking for** somewhere to rent.
9. People with disabilities encounter difficulties in **discovering / finding** jobs.
10. She has **found / found out** the man of her dreams.
11. The police are **looking for / searching for** the criminal.
12. We had some difficulty **finding / finding out** his house.
13. We have been **finding out / discovering / searching for** an antidote for seven years.
14. I will **find / find out** who did this.
15. We're **looking for / finding / searching for** a missing young girl - the situation is desperate.

1) found out / discovered 2) looking for 3) find, find / look for 4) found 5) searched, find 6) looked for 7) find out 8) looking for 9) finding 10) found 11) searching for 12) finding 13) searching 14) find out 15) searching for

Chapter 33
Fit, Match, Suit, Go Well With

Red is a color that fits me very well.
Red is a color that **suits** me very well.
The jacket doesn't match the shirt.
The jacket doesn't **go with** the shirt.
This wine is great but it doesn't fit well with white meat.
This wine is great but it doesn't **go well with** well with white meat.

> These shoes **fit** me perfectly.
>
> She **fits** the description of the murderer.
>
> That jacket really **suits** you - you look great in it.
>
> Which of these shoes would **go best with** this dress?
>
> I need the right color cardigan to **match** my dress.
>
> I work part time, which **suits** me very well.

Guidelines

- **fit** - be the right size
- **suit** - look appropriate, look good
- **match** - be harmonious with, correspond in some essential way
- **go well with** – look / taste good in combination with something else

Choose the correct form

1. The sofa didn't **fit / match** anywhere.
2. Several people seem to **match / suit** the description of the criminal.
3. People work together when it **goes well with / suits** them.
4. Those shoes don't **match / fit** your dress.
5. That jacket doesn't **fit / suit** you - it's way too big.
6. This color **goes / suits / matches** well with lots of things.
7. It **fits / suits** you well, you look younger.
8. That attitude doesn't **fit / match / suit** you very well.
9. Some of my son's old clothes will probably **fit / match / suit** you - you are about the same size.
10. That blue would really **fit / match / suit** your eyes.
11. It is clear that misunderstandings arise when politicians say what **goes well with / suits** them rather than giving the full facts.
12. The punishment should have **fitted / suited** the perceived crime.
13. But he doesn't **fit / match / suit** the profile. He's not the type of person we are looking for.
14. I think she **fits / matches / suits** you perfectly - she's just your kind of woman.

1. The sofa didn't **fit** anywhere.
2. Several people seem to **match** the description of the criminal.
3. People work together when it **suits** them.
4. Those shoes don't **match** your dress.
5. That jacket doesn't **fit** you - it's way too big.
6. This color **goes** well with lots of things.
7. It **suits** you well, you look younger
8. That attitude doesn't **suit** you very well.
9. Some of my son's old clothes will probably **fit** you - you are about the same size.
10. That blue would really **match** your eyes.
11. It is clear that misunderstandings arise when politicians say what **suits** them rather than giving the full facts.
12. The punishment should have **fitted** the perceived crime.
13. But he doesn't **fit** the profile. He's not the type of person we are looking for.
14. I think she **suits** you perfectly - she's just your kind of woman.

Chapter 34
Grow, Grow Up, Increase, Cultivate

Many children grow in an atmosphere of violence.

Many children **grow up** in an atmosphere of violence.

We need to go back to the time when mothers stayed at home growing children.

We need to go back to the time when mothers stayed at home **bringing up / raising** children.

My mother was grown in Warsaw.

My mother **grew up** in Warsaw.

Our olive oil production grows every year.

Our olive oil production **increases** every year.

We **grow** tomatoes and carrots in our vegetable garden.

My little boy has **grown** 10 cm in the last month.

The company has **grown** considerably - last year we had 5 employees, now we have 50.

Said to a 10 year old boy: Wow you have **grown** a lot since I last saw you. Look how tall you are!

She has **grownup** a lot since I last saw her. She is much more mature and like an adult.

I **grew up** in Manchester. I was born and educated there. My parents looked after me and taught me things.

I was **brought up / raised** a Catholic.

We don't want to **raise** our family here in a polluted town, so we are moving to the country.

Guidelines

- **grow** = increase in size, volume, height (people and things)
- **increase** = become bigger in size, volume (things only)
- **grow** = cultivate vegetables and flowers (note: you cannot 'grow' a garden)
- **cultivate** - farmland; promote / instill metaphorically
- **grow up** = spend your childhood, to mature
- **bring up, raise** = educate one's children at home or in a certain place
- **be brought up, be raised** - spend one's childhood in a certain place and in a certain way

Choose the correct form

1. They **grew / grew up** in rural Vermont and were **grown / raised** by two god-fearing parents.
2. I **brought up / grew up** playing the violin. My parents **cultivated / grew** a passion for music in me.
3. This was my favorite book **bringing up / growing up**. It's about a child who was **grown / raised** by wolves.
4. I'm trying to **grow up / raise** these kids by myself.
5. Look how the garden has **grown / grown up**. But this doesn't mean that we need to **increase / grow** the amount of insecticides we use.
6. The festival has **grown / grown up** over the years to where it now rivals some of the big ones - the number of people who come has **raised / increased** from a couple of hundred in the first year to over 10,000.
7. I wanted to **cultivate / grow** a beard to make me look more **grown up / raised**. I had such a baby face.
8. It is important that we **cultivate / grow** and preserve this multiculturalism.
9. I have spent three years **cultivating / growing** the perfect garden.
10. We've seen each other's kids **grow up / bring up**. We both **brought / grew** them up with the same values.

1) grew up, raised 2) grew up, cultivated 3) growing up, raised 4) raise 5) grown 6) grown, increased 7) grow, grown up 8) cultivate 9) cultivating 10) grow up, brought

Chapter 35
Happen, Occur, Take Place

The seminar will occur at 09.00 tomorrow.

The seminar will **take place** at 09.00 tomorrow.

A fire happened at the school over the weekend.

There was a fire at the school over the weekend.

An accident was happened outside my house.

An accident **happened / There was** an accident outside my house.

Did there happen something strange?

Did something strange **happen**?

It happened / succeeded the same thing to me.

The same thing **happened** to me.

What has happened with you?

What has happened **to** you?

It may happen that I get drunk at parties.

I **occasionally / sometimes** get drunk at parties.

The art historians thought it was a Van Gogh, but it occurred that it was a fake.

The art historians thought it was a Van Gogh, but it **turned out** to be a fake.

What we occur to overcome this challenge is a new strategy.

What we **need** to overcome this challenge is a new strategy.

Errors often **occur** as a result of human incompetence.

Why do these things just seem to **happen** to me and not anyone else?

What's **happened** to you? You look terrible.

A total lunar eclipse **occurs / happens** when the moon and the sun are on exact opposite sides of Earth.

The disease tends to **occur** in children only late in life.

The plant **occurs** naturally throughout most of East Africa.

Meetings **take place** on a monthly basis.

Guidelines

- **happen** = unplanned events, encounter something by chance, make a chance appearance
- **take place** = planned events
- **occur** = unplanned events (formal, often in a natural or medical context)
- **occur to someone** = come to mind

Choose the correct form. In some cases, there may be more than one correct form

1. Another meeting **occurred / took place** on 28 November 2023.
2. I mean, it could **occur / happen** to anyone.
3. It **happened / occurred** to me that you might need some advice.
4. Loss of appetite may **occur / take place** during treatment.
5. The police said the shooting **happened / took place** outside a bar in Main Street.
6. The seminar is **occurring / taking place** next month instead of next week.
7. This all **happened / took place** a long time ago.
8. Well, I **happened / occurred** to be in the neighborhood so I thought I would come by and say hello.
9. Mutations can **happen / occur** at any time and anywhere.
10. What do you think **will happen / occur** next?
11. What **happened / took place** last night? Did you win the match?

1) took place 2) happen 3) occurred 4) occur 5) happened / took place 6) taking place 7) happened / took place 8) happened 9) occur 10) will happen 11) happened

Chapter 36
Home, House; Homework, Housework

Our home is next door to a cinema.

Our **house** is next door to a cinema.

When I returned to house I found that the door had been broken.

When I returned **home** I found that the door had been broken.

His house is an apartment.

He lives in an apartment.

When I arrived at home I had a shower.

When I arrived **home** I had a shower.

We don't have any time to do the home work so we have hired a cleaner.

We don't have any time to do the **housework** so we have hired a cleaner.

Don't give us too many homeworks.

Don't give us too much **homework**.

> You have a lovely **home** - I like the atmosphere you have created with your furnishing.
>
> You have a lovely **house** - I love the brickwork on the outside, and all the shutters on the windows.
>
> They've painted their **house** white.
>
> Pete is **at home** already, and Kate is coming **home** later.
>
> I do all the **housework** and she does all the cooking.
>
> My children often forget to do their **homework** for school.

Guidelines

- **house** - physical building
- **home** - the place where you live, the atmosphere and feel of where you live
- **go / return / come back home, be at home**
- **homework** (uncountable noun) - exercises for school
- **housework** (uncountable noun) - cleaning and tidying

Some sentences are correct, others are not. Correct the incorrect sentences.

1. I usually leave my house every morning at about 7 am.
2. Tonight I'm going to a friend's home for dinner.
3. I bought my house about 5 years ago, it wasn't very expensive.
4. At the weekend I hate doing homework, especially cleaning the floors.
5. I'm doing an English course at the moment and our teachers gives us lots of homeworks.
6. Are you going home or are you staying here? I am going to home.
7. I am moving house.
8. He goes to his home for his lunch every day.
9. He goes to his girlfriend's house for lunch.
10. They have a big house in the country.
11. I want to live near my parents' home.
12. We are building a house.
13. He is not at home at the moment.
14. It is a nice room in a nice home.
15. Our home is on the first floor.

1. I usually leave **home** every morning at about 7 am.
2. Tonight I'm going to a friend's **house** for dinner.
3. OK
4. At the weekend I hate doing **housework**, especially cleaning the floors.
5. I'm doing an English course at the moment and our teachers gives us lots of **homework**.
6. Are you going home or are you staying here? I am **going home**.
7. OK
8. He **goes home** for his lunch every day.
9. OK
10. OK
11. I want to live near my **parents' (house)**.
12. OK
13. OK
14. It is a nice room in a nice **flat / apartment / house**.
15. Our **flat / apartment** is on the first floor.

Chapter 37
In the End, At the End, Eventually, Finally, At Last, Lastly, If Necessary

At the end there was nothing we could do about it. We'd tried everything.

In the end there was nothing we could do about it. We'd tried everything.

They came at the end having made me wait nearly three hours.

Eventually / In the end they came, having made me wait nearly three hours.

At last, I want to say that …

Finally / Lastly, I want to say that …

First we listened to some music, then we watched a move, and at last we went to bed.

First we listened to some music, then we watched a move, and **finally** we went to bed.

He comes eventually.

He **may** come.

Some viewers may find the movie eventually shocking.

Some viewers **may** find the movie shocking.

Stop crying at last and tell me what happened.

It's time to stop crying and tell me what happened.

> **At the end** of the movie / book / lesson, I felt exhilarated.
>
> We couldn't decide where to go on holiday, so **in the end** we stayed at home.
>
> Firstly we need to do x, secondly we need to do y, and **finally / lastly** we need to do z.
>
> This information remained confidential for 50 years, full details **finally** came to light only in 2018.
>
> This information remained confidential for 50 years but **in the end** pressure from the public forced the government to reveal the horrifying truth.
>
> **At last / Finally**, someone who really understands this kind of music.
>
> We can take the high road and **if necessary** stop at a service station for lunch.

Guidelines

- **in the end / eventually** - after a lot of difficulties
- **at the end** - refers to the final part of a road, movie, book, lesson
- **finally / lastly** - to introduce last item in a list / last event in a sequence
- **at last** - used as an exclamation
- **if necessary** - in case we need to

Choose the correct form

1. I knew someone would come **eventually / finally / lastly**.
2. Sometimes **at the end / in the end** of the day I feel I have achieved nothing.
3. We wanted to go to Paris but **at the end / in the end / lastly** we had to settle for Prague.
4. **In the end / Eventually / If necessary** we decided to abandon the tests.
5. If we carry on using resources indiscriminately, **eventually / at the end / in the end** there will be no resources left.
6. **At the end / In the end** of the lesson our teacher told us some jokes.
7. She didn't seem all that surprised **at the end / in the end / finally**.
8. Despite the health warnings, many patients had continued smoking for several years before **eventually / in the end / lastly** stopping.
9. **Eventually / If necessary / Finally** a more expensive solution can be used.
10. I figured you'd show up here **eventually / finally / if necessary**.
11. And **at the end / in the end / finally** we decided we liked London the best.
12. **Finally / At last / In the end** I would like to thank everyone who helped me make this dream come true.
13. All of us must face this truth **at the end / lastly / eventually**.
14. **Finally / Lastly / At last!** You've here!

1) eventually 2) at the end 3) in the end 4) in the end (eventually) 5) eventually (in the end) 6) at the end 7) in the end 8) eventually 9) If necessary 10) eventually 11) in the end 12) finally 13) eventually 14) at last

Chapter 38
Job, Work

She has two works - mother and housewife.

She has two **jobs** - mother and housewife.

This is a work for an expert.

This is a **job** for an expert.

This will take a long time - it's a hard work.

This will take a long time - it's **hard work**.

The company has created 10 new workplaces.

The company has created 10 new **jobs**.

I must do a work for my English teacher.

I must do a **piece of work / some work / some task / some exercise** for my English teacher.

She is employed in the same company as him.

She **works** for the same company as him.

He's got a **job** as an intern in a bank.

We've got a lot of **jobs** to do today. We need to fix the computer, do those photocopies and write up the report.

It's not my **job** to clean up after your parties.

Well done, you've done a really good **job**.

Studying this astrophysics book is hard **work**.

Things aren't going very well at **work** at the moment.

Is the **job / work** interesting at the new place?

What kind of **job / work** do you do?

Safety in the **workplace** is of primary importance to us.

Guidelines

- **job** - countable noun, refers to a paid occupation, or a task, duty or responsibility
- **work** - uncountable, refers to a mass of undefined tasks, or to one's place of occupation
- **works** - collection of literary or artistic pieces; road works
- **workplace** - environment where someone works

Some sentences are correct, others are not. Correct the incorrect sentences

1. Although it's not really the job I was looking for, I enjoy most of the work involved.
2. Creating work at a time of unemployment is essential - we need to create at least 100 a month.
3. The merger between the two companies will eliminate at least 20,000 workplaces.
4. Financing the work ahead is a major challenge.
5. He does two works.
6. He paid me, I needed the job.
7. He spends more time at work than at home.
8. He's trying to find a work.
9. I go to job at 9.
10. I haven't accepted the job yet - I am still waiting to see if I get any better offers.
11. I saw myself doing the job.
12. I'm looking for a job as a dolphin trainer.
13. It was an interesting work.
14. She's always talking about job.
15. Temporary jobs can only partly compensate for this.
16. This is the work of a professional - beautifully executed. You have to admire some criminals.
17. We're doing some works on the house.
18. You did a good work.
19. Shakespeare's collected works cost around $15 for a cheap edition.
20. The roadworks caused a 3 km long traffic jam.

1) OK 2) jobs 3) jobs 4) OK 5) jobs 6) work 7) OK 8) job 9) work 10) OK 11) OK 12) OK 13) it was an interesting job / it was interesting work 14) work 15) OK 16) OK 17) work 18) job 19) OK 20) OK

Chapter 39
Know, Meet

I have known him at a party.

I **met** him at a party.

He wants to travel so that he can know other people.

He wants to travel so that he can **meet** other people.

By working in an office, you know a lot of people.

By working in an office, you **get to know** a lot of people.

She didn't go in the sea, because she didn't know swimming.

She didn't go in the sea, because she doesn't **know how to** swim.

The best way to know a city is to visit it on foot.

The best way to **get to know / discover** a city is to visit it on foot.

At the party I knew many new friends.

At the party I **made** many new friends.

I have known you are leaving soon - I am really sorry.

I have **heard** you are leaving soon - I am really sorry.

I don't know English very well.

I don't **speak** English very well.

> Have you **known** them for a long time or did you **meet** them recently?
>
> When you **meet** a person for the first time how long does it take for you to make an impression of them?
>
> When you **know** a person really well do you feel able to ask them absolutely anything?
>
> How long does it usually take you to **get to know** someone sufficiently well that you can trust them?
>
> He still doesn't **know how to** tie his shoelaces.
>
> This **meets** all my needs and priorities.

Guidelines

- **know someone** - to have spent time with someone of several occasions
- **meet someone** - make contact with someone for the first time; arrange an appointment with someone
- **get to know someone** - improve your knowledge and understanding of someone over a period of time
- **know how to** - have the knowledge and capacity to do something
- **meet** - satisfy requirements

Choose the correct form

1. I **met / knew / got to know** him 20 years ago so I have **known / met** him for a long time.
2. I don't think I have **known / met** you before.
3. We can be satisfied that key priorities have been **known / met**.
4. I have **known / met** a lot of Italians in London, many of them own restaurants.
5. Before I make any decisions, I would like to **know / get to know** you better.
6. We have been **meeting / getting to know** in secret for some time now.
7. All my demands have been **known / met**.
8. The underlying facts have been **known / met** for years.
9. They had **known / met** each other since university.
10. After we had **met / known / got to know** them a couple of times, they invited us for dinner at their house, where we **knew / got to know** them much better.
11. I'm so glad that you came to **know / meet** us at the airport.
12. The man who tried to shoot you, did you **know** him?
13. It takes a while to **know / get to know** her, she's very shy.
14. Do you **know / know how to** play the violin?

1) met, known 2) met 3) met 4) met 5) get to know 6) meeting [getting to know each other], 7) met 8) known 9) known 10) met, got to know 11) meet 12) know 13) get to know 14) know how to

Chapter 40
Last, Latest, Most Recent; Next, the Next

Have you read his last novel?

Have you read his **latest** novel?

The latest election was won by the Republicans.

The **last** election was won by the Republicans.

She arrived the last week.

She arrived **last** week.

I didn't sleep well this night.

I didn't sleep well **last** night.

Last evening we went to the movies.

Yesterday we went to the movies.

On last Saturday we went to the movies.

Last Saturday we went to the movies.

In the last time houses prices have been going up dramatically.

Recently, houses prices have been going up dramatically.

I am very busy in this period / in these days.

I have been very busy **recently / in the last few days**. / I am very busy **at the moment**.

> His **last** movie (i.e. the one before the one that is now showing at the cinema) was terrible, but his **latest** movie (the one at cinemas now) has had great reviews.
>
> 'Eyes Wide Shut' (1999) was Stanley Kubrick's **last** film. (Kubrick is dead)
>
> **Last** week I went to hospital to have my tonsils removed. (*last week* = the week before this week)
>
> I am going back to New York in **the last week** of December. (*the last week* = a specific week in the future or the past)
>
> In **the last few weeks** I have been going to the cinema a lot. (*in the last few weeks* = from the recent past until now)
>
> I will see him **next week**. (i.e. the week after this week)
>
> I am going to England **next week** and then the following week I am going to Spain.
>
> I will be working hard in **the next few weeks.** (= starting from today for 3-4 weeks)

Guidelines

- **last** - the time before the current one (e.g. the week before the current week); the final one
- **the last** - a specific time in the past or the future
- **in the last <u>few</u>** + days, weeks, months etc
- **latest** = the most recent (possibly in a series that is likely to continue)

Note: The rules for *last* and *the last* are also applicable to *next* and *the next*.

1. In the first week everything was OK, but in **next / the next** two weeks everything began to go wrong.
2. I want to share with you my **last / latest** art project.
3. Have you heard the **last / latest**? They're getting married next spring.
4. I am always the **last / latest** person to know.
5. I wouldn't marry him even if he was the **last / latest** person on earth.
6. In **the last few / the last** years of his life he became a recluse.
7. OK this time you did it really badly. **Next / The next** time I want you do to it really well.
8. According to the **last / latest** statistics, five million people here suffer from diabetes.
9. See you **next / the next** Thursday!
10. That's **the last / latest** thing I want to do.
11. **Next / The next** time you see her can you send her my love?
12. Have you met her **last / latest** boyfriend? He's really nice.
13. The pain should wear off in **the next few / the next** hours.
14. This could be the **last / latest** time I see her - she's going to live in Australia.
15. TV journalist: I'm at the scene of his **last / latest** attack.

1) the next 2) latest 3) latest 4) last 5) last 6) the last few 7) next 8) latest 9) next 10) the last 11) next / the next 12) latest 13) the next few 14) last 15) latest

Chapter 41
Look At, See, Watch

We looked at a movie on Netflix.

We **watched** a movie on Netflix.

We spent the day watching paintings at the modern art museum.

We spent the day **looking at** paintings at the modern art museum.

She had a quick look on her watch and decided to leave.

She had a quick **look at** her watch and decided to leave.

I don't face to face with my neighbors.

I rarely **see** my neighbors.

When I was young I liked watching comics.

When I was young I liked **reading** comics.

You see pale today.

You **look** pale today.

Teacher, have you seen our tests yet?

Teacher, have you **marked** our tests yet?

> **Watch** me, I'm going to show you how to dance the samba.
>
> Aren't you going to **watch** TV tonight?
>
> I went to an electrical shop to **look at** TVs. I bought the biggest one and then **watched** movies all night.
>
> You are **looking** in the wrong direction, it's over there not here.
>
> Will you **look at** me when I'm talking to you?
>
> **Look at** the stars – how beautiful they are tonight.
>
> **Can** you **see** my pen anywhere?
>
> I **couldn't see** you from here.

Guidelines

- **look (at)** - observe. There is little or no sense of movement
- **see** - is a verb of the senses and refers to one's physical sight. It is generally used with *can* with this meaning. It also means think, perceive, judge; have an appointment
- **watch** - used for things that are moving (people, images on film, shows, TV, sports); take care of, control, check on

1. I was **looking / seeing / watching** in the other direction, obviously.
2. I **looked / saw / watched** this video on YouTube last night.
3. I am **looking / seeing / watching** the doctor tomorrow.
4. I'll be **looking / seeing / watching** you, Pete, so be careful.
5. I'll **look / see / watch** you on Saturday then - and by the way don't be late, the match starts at 3.0.
6. The fact that you're even **looking / looking at / watching** my photos without my permission makes me really angry.
7. Just **looking / looking at / watching** you in that hoodie makes me worried.
8. He was **looking / seeing / watching** all around and then he saw me.
9. A performance audit **looks at / looks** the quality and results of management.
10. I can **see / look / watch** your house from here.
11. I miss the way she **looks / looks at / watches** me.
12. I thought you were **looking / seeing / watching** the game with my dad.
13. I don't **look / see / watch** you as being an accountant, an artist maybe.
14. I **look / see / watch** you in a very different light, now that you have told me the whole truth.

1) looking 2) watched 3) seeing 4) watching 5) see 6) looking at 7) looking at 8) looking 9) looks at 10) see 11) looks 12) watching 13) see 14) see

Chapter 42
Look, Seem, Sound

It looks a good idea.

It **seems like / sounds like** a good idea.

He looks an English man.

He **looks like** an English man.

You look like nervous.

You **look** nervous.

I heard a noise that sounded to be a child crying.

I heard a noise that **sounded like** a child crying.

Your house looks wonderfully.

Your house **looks wonderful**.

My accent in English doesn't sound well.

My accent in English doesn't **sound good**.

> You **look** tired today.
>
> The man on the left **looks** English.
>
> The man on the left **looks like** an English man.
>
> It **looks** as if it's going to rain.
>
> Everyone was so happy, it seemed **like** a party.
>
> He doesn't **seem** to understand much.
>
> Listen. It **sounds** like a mouse.
>
> From what you've said your idea **sounds** really useful.

Guidelines

- **look** + adjective, **look like** + noun - physical impressions and appearances
- **seem** + adjective, **seem like** + noun - intuitions and atmospheres
- **sound** + adjective, **sound like** + noun - noises, someone's voice or to musical styles

Note: *feel* and *taste* follow the same guidelines.

Choose the correct form

1. A reference written by you would **look / look like** great on my LinkedIn page.
2. It **looks / seems** incredible how little you get paid.
3. She **looks / seems** gorgeous.
4. She **looks / seems / looks like / seems like** as if she might be about to be sick.
5. It **looks / seems / sounds** strange that he speaks such good English when he has never been there.
6. It **seems like / looks like** a good idea but maybe it isn't.
7. This music **seems like / sounds like** the Beatles.
8. He **sounded / sounded like** a bit angry on the phone.
9. It **seemed like / looked like** something you should know.
10. I've been **looking / watching** you for some time now and you're **looking / seeming** really strange.
11. You **looked / sounded** strange on the phone, your voice was trembling.
12. He **looks / seems** as if he is going to cry.
13. Your face **looks like / seems like** a battlefield.
14. This will **sound like / look like** a highly improbable story.
15. It **sounds / sounds like** stupid, but it's really funny.
16. It **looked / seemed like** a good idea at the time.
17. You **looked / seemed** good the other night.

1) look 2) seems 3) looks 4) looks 5) seems 6) seems like 7) sounds like 8) sounded 9) seemed like 10) watching, looking 11) sounded 12) looks 13) looks like 14) sound like 15) sounds 16) seemed like 17) looked

Chapter 43
Lose, Lack, Miss, Waste

I don't want to lose any more time doing this stupid exercise.

I don't want to **waste** any more time doing this stupid exercise.

He misses intelligence.

He **lacks** intelligence. / He is **lacking** in intelligence.

In emails the tone of voice is missing.

Email **lacks** any tone of voice.

Have you finished the test? I am missing the last question.

I **haven't done** the last question yet.

She has three exams missing.

She **still** has three exams **to do**.

I was missing at the last lesson.

I **missed** the lesson / I **didn't come** to the last lesson.

Our country lacks of care for the homeless.

In our country **there is a lack** of care for the homeless.

I have to loose weight / to lose my weight.

I have to **lose** weight.

> I've **missed** three lectures so far this month.
>
> We **missed** the first train so we had to catch the later one.
>
> Three people are **missing** on the mountain.
>
> I can't find my wallet. I must have **lost** it.
>
> Don't **waste** time doing those exercises.
>
> He's **wasted** a lot of money buying useless objects.
>
> She **lacks / is lacking** motivation.
>
> You **lack** faith - you really need to believe in this project.

Guidelines

- **miss** - fail to be present or to be late when something happens; usually used with transport, appointments and opportunities. *miss* is not used to say that someone hasn't got something
- **lack, be lacking** - be without, not have a sufficient amount
- **lose** - not have anymore; generally used with objects and money
- **waste** - consume unnecessarily, typically used with time, resources and energy

Choose the correct form

1. I'm sorry but you're **losing / missing** the point and I am beginning to **lose / miss** my patience.
2. I realized I had **lost / wasted** the first 20 years of my adult life with the wrong person.
3. There are two pictures are **lacking / missing** from this room - someone has stolen them.
4. This room **lacks / misses** pictures - there are no pictures at all.
5. I **lack / miss** you, I can't wait to see you again.
6. You **lost / missed** a great party.
7. Her parents have basically **lacked / lost** control of her.
8. It has now been realized that several items are **lacking / missing** from the museum and suspicions have been raised that these items might actually have been stolen.
9. The museum is **lacking / missing** a section on Egyptology, and the curators are now discussing setting up a small collection of Egyptian artifacts.
10. The store's been **losing / wasting** money for years, despite making some great improvements.
11. Unfortunately it looks like we are going to **lack / miss** the deadline.
12. It is clear from his behavior that the child **lacks / misses** his mother.
13. My laptop is **lacking / missing** - has someone put it somewhere?
14. I may have **lost / missed** my opportunity and I don't want to **lose / waste** energy talking to you about it.

1) missing, lose 2) wasted 3) missing 4) lacks 5) miss 6) missed 7) lost 8) missing 9) lacking 10) losing 11) miss 12) misses 13) missing 14) missed, waste

Chapter 44
Remember, Remind, Forget

I remind the holidays we spent together.

I **remember** the holidays we spent together.

I don't want to be remembered that it is my birthday today.

I don't want to be **reminded** that it is my birthday today.

I would like to remember you that we need the doc by the end of this week.

I would like to **remind** you that we need the doc by the end of this week.

I did not remember to meet them before, but I pretended I knew them.

I did not **remember meeting** them before, but I pretended I knew them.

As I remember, you prefer red wine to white.

I **seem to remember** that you prefer red wine to white.

I suddenly memorized that I had a dentist's appointment.

I suddenly **remembered** that I had a dentist's appointment.

He forgot his homework at home.

He **left** his homework at home.

I can never **remember** his name. I keep **forgetting** it.

Please **remind** me to give you the photocopies at the end of the lesson.

You **remind** me of my mother. You have a very similar way of smiling.

Please **remember to tell** him about the meeting - don't **forget**!

I **remember telling** him about the meeting = I **remember** the moment in which I told him because his shocked face clearly showed he had completely **forgotten** about it.

I think I must have **left** my phone at the party.

Guidelines

- **remember (to do something)** - not forget to do something
- **remember doing something** - recall the moment when something was happening
- **remind someone to do something** - say something to ensure someone does not forget
- **remind me / you / her etc of something** - make yourself or someone think about something that typically you have seen or heard before
- **forget (to do something)** - fail to remember
- **leave** - misplace an object

Some sentences are correct, others are not. Correct the incorrect sentences.

1. Remember me to buy milk.
2. You remember me my ex boyfriend.
3. I forgot studying last night.
4. I'd like to remember you that your homework is due in tomorrow.
5. Now try to remember how you felt when we were here.
6. I have a hard time remembering these things.
7. I will never forget you Julia.
8. Honey, I didn't forget to call. I just couldn't get through.
9. And don't forget to put the alarm on when you leave.
10. I remember drawing these because I didn't want to forget any details.
11. This reminds me my mother's cooking.
12. It might remind you of home or something.
13. You'll be pleased to know that I remembered going to the post office for you.
14. She forgot her bag on the train.
15. This music remembers me the Beatles.

1) **Remind** me to buy milk. 2) You **remind me of** my ex boyfriend. 3) I forgot **to study** last night.
4) I'd like to **remind** you that your homework is due in tomorrow. 5-10) OK
11) This **reminds me of** my mother's cooking. 12) OK
13) You'll be pleased to know that I remembered **to go** to the post office for you.
14) She **left** her bag on the train. 15) This music **reminds me of** the Beatles.

Chapter 45
Rise, Arise, Raise

Buy now - they will probably rise the cost of the seats as the holidays gets closer.

Buy now - they will probably **raise** the cost of the seats as the holidays gets closer.

The sun raises in the east.

The sun **rises** in the east.

I am hoping my boss will rise my salary.

I am hoping my boss will **raise** my salary.

My salary has not raised with inflation.

My salary has not **risen** with inflation.

A problem has rised.

A problem has **arisen**.

> The sun **rises** in the east and sets in the west.
>
> Last month the share index **rose** by 25 points.
>
> I'm afraid that various problems have **arisen**.
>
> The government have **raised** taxes.
>
> This issue has never been **raised** before by any of our clients. You are the first to **raise** it.
>
> She **raised** several points during the lecture.
>
> This issue has never **arisen** before - we are not sure why it happened.

Guidelines

- **rise** (rose, risen) - intransitive - refers to involuntary actions (to go up, to reach a higher level)
- **arise** (arose, arisen) - same meaning as *rise* but in a figurative sense
- **raise** - transitive - refers to voluntary actions (to increase, to make higher, to propose, to lift)

Choose the correct form

1. The government is planning to **arise / raise / rise** taxes in the hope that this will stop inflation from **arising / raising / rising** further.
2. They **arose / rose / raised** the building using a crane. Several issues **arose / raised / rose** while the building was **arising / raising / rising** upwards.
3. Inflation could have **arisen / raised / risen** to 12% if the Central Bank had not intervened.
4. Inflation has **arisen / raised / risen**. Social problems have **arisen / raised / risen** due to the consequent high levels of unemployment, which has **arisen / raised / risen** the level of violence throughout the country.
5. Some clients have **arisen / raised / risen** several issues with regard to the use of English. These issues seem to have **arisen / raised / risen** from the fact that there are a considerable number of grammatical errors. In fact the number of such complaints about our documents has **arisen / raised / risen** dramatically.
6. She **arose / raised / rose** her arm to ask a question.
7. We then estimated that the unemployment rate would have **arisen / raised / risen** by 15% or more if those measures had not been introduced.
8. Let us **arise / raise / rise** our glasses in a toast to our distinguished guest.
9. We are hoping to **arise / raise / rise** awareness of this issue.
10. Similar situations have **arisen / raised / risen** in the past for weeks, and the number is **arising / raising / rising** rapidly.

1) raise, rising 2) rose, arose, rising 3) risen 4) risen, arisen, raised 5) raised, arisen, risen 6) raised 7) risen 8) raise 9) raise 10) arisen, rising

Chapter 46
Say, Tell

Can you say me where the station is?

Can you **tell** me where the station is?

He told: "I love you".

He **said**: "I love you".

I said her that I loved her.

I **told** her that I loved her. / I **said** that I loved her.

Please tell Anna "hello".

Please say "hello" to Anna.

She told that the movie was not very good.

She **told me / said** that the movie was not very good.

I was said to report to you for instructions.

I was **told** to report to you for instructions.

Do we have to say about what we think?

Do we have to **talk about** what we think? Do we have to **say** ..? Do we have to **tell** you ...

> I **said**: "You should study more". = I **told them** to study more.
>
> He **said** that he loved me. = He **told me** that he loved me.
>
> **Tell my mother** that I will be arriving late.
>
> Don't **say** anything.
>
> **Say** 'hello' to Andrea for me.
>
> She **told (us)** a good joke / story about ...

Guidelines

- **say** + something (to someone) - to report the exact words, either in direct or indirect speech
- **say** + *that* - to report the exact words
- **tell** + someone (*that* / something / to do something)- indirect speech
- **tell** + stories, jokes

Choose the correct form

1. We'll **say to / tell** them tonight about what happened.
2. **Say / tell** that again.
3. I can't understand what he's **saying / telling**.
4. He **said / told us** to go home.
5. He **said / told** nothing funny.
6. She **said / told** him that he was wrong.
7. They **said / told** some terrible stories about their childhood.
8. She **said / told** "I think we should leave now".
9. The doctor **said / told** the patient not to worry about the operation.
10. The prime minister **said / told** she would reduce unemployment.
11. She **said / told** "here you are" and gave me a thousand dollars.
12. They didn't **say / tell** anything interesting.
13. They didn't **say / tell** us anything that we didn't know already.
14. **Say / Tell** them that the lesson begins at 9.00.
15. I **said / told** 'why' not 'what'.
16. What did you **say / tell**? I didn't hear you.

1) tell 2) say 3) saying 4) told us 5) said 6) told 7) told 8) said 9) told 10) said 11) said 12) say 13) tell 14) tell 15) said 16) say

Chapter 47
Sorry, Excuse, Apologize

He asked the teacher if he could be pardoned for a few minutes while he made a phone call.

He asked the teacher if he could be **excused** for a few minutes while he made a phone call.

I apologized myself for being late.

I **apologized** for being late.

I really sorry about what happened.

I **am really sorry** about what happened.

Could you excuse me at the meeting tomorrow?

Could you **apologize on my behalf** that I won't be at the meeting tomorrow?

Sorry, what did you say?

Sorry I am late.

Excuse me, what did you say?

Excuse me, do you know where the station is?

Please **excuse** my husband's behavior - he's drunk.

I **apologize** for my husband's behavior.

Guidelines

- **apologize** to someone for doing something - making an apology / express regret for something that you have done wrong
- **(to be) sorry (about)** - to apologize
- **excuse me** - to apologize for having done something; before asking or interrupting someone
- **excuse** someone for something

Decide in which cases both forms in bold are correct, and in which cases only one form is correct.

1. You do not need to **apologize / say you are sorry**, you have done nothing wrong.
2. I've been sitting here trying to think of ways to **apologize / excuse** to you.
3. I **was very sorry / apologize** to hear about your friend.
4. Please **apologize / excuse** my son, he's only six and is very excited about all this.
5. **Excuse / Sorry,** we need to talk in private.
6. I **am sorry / I apologize** that it has taken me so long to get back to you.
7. **I'm sorry, excuse me / Please excuse me** one second.
8. **Sorry to bother you / Excuse me**, but please could you help with these heavy bags.
9. If you could **be sorry about / excuse** me for a moment, I need to answer this call.
10. I **apologize / am sorry** for accusing you wrongly.
11. I am incredibly **excuse / sorry** about what happened.
12. **Sorry to interrupt / Excuse me for interrupting** your lesson, but could I have a word with you for a second?

1. You do not need to **apologize / say you are sorry**, you have done nothing wrong.
2. I've been sitting here trying to think of ways to **apologize** to you.
3. I **was very sorry** to hear about your friend.
4. Please **excuse** my son, he's only six and is very excited about all this.
5. **Sorry,** we need to talk in private.
6. I **am sorry / I apologize** that it has taken me so long to get back to you.
7. **I'm sorry, excuse me / Please excuse me** one second.
8. **Sorry to bother you / Excuse me**, but please could you help with these heavy bags.
9. If you could **excuse** me for a moment, I need to answer this call.
10. I **apologize / am sorry** for accusing you wrongly.
11. I am incredibly **sorry** about what happened.
12. **Sorry to interrupt / Excuse me for interrupting** your lesson,

Chapter 48
Think, Think Of, Think About, Believe

A: She will come. B: I believe that too.

A: She will come. B: I **think so** too.

I believed she was a police officer.

I **thought** she was a police officer.

What do you think about? I am thinking to my mother.

What **are you thinking** about? I am **thinking about** my mother.

Do you believe that they will come?

Do you **think** that they will come?

I am thinking to go to Thailand.

I am thinking **of going** to Thailand.

I think he didn't understand.

I **don't think** he understood.

If you mean nothing is impossible, try getting a ticket to Lorde's concert.

If you **think** nothing is impossible, try getting a ticket to Lorde's concert.

In my opinion, I think you should see a doctor.

I **think** you should see a doctor.

> What **do you think** about climate change? What's your real opinion?
>
> What do you **think of / about** our new boss? What do you think he is like?
>
> What **are you thinking** about? What is on your mind?
>
> We are **thinking about** going on holiday to France.
>
> When I **think about** my life I realize how lucky I am.
>
> What do you **think of** me? Do you like me, or hate me?
>
> I don't **think much of** this book. I don't really like it and it's badly written.
>
> I **believe** you when you say you felt something strange. But I personally don't **believe** in ghosts.

Guidelines

- **think of** - have an opinion
- **think about** - reflect on something, have an opinion
- **I (don't) think so** - believe that something is (not) true
- **believe** - have a strong opinion about, trust, have faith in

Some sentences are correct, others are not. Correct the incorrect sentences.

1. Is Elena coming to the party? Yes, at least I think.
2. When I was a kid, I thought adults always told the truth.
3. I think it's not important.
4. I am thinking to go there tomorrow.
5. I think at her all day long. I miss her so much.
6. I've been thinking a lot about you.
7. I've been thinking it over and I am thinking that you may be right after all.
8. Jim thought no one would ever look for us here.
9. I just didn't think you'd ever want to see me again.
10. I can't believe you would do this to me.
11. I used to believe Coldplay were good.
12. I actually believed the things you said.
13. I know what you all are thinking right now.
14. At the moment you are thinking like a politician, try thinking like a normal human being.
15. Will she come to the party? I think yes.

1) Yes, at least I think **so**. 2) OK 3) I **don't think it's** important. 4) I am thinking **of / about going** there tomorrow. 5) I think **about** her. 6) OK 7) I **think** that you may be right after all. 8) OK 9) OK 10) OK 11) think 12) OK 13) OK 14) OK 15) I think **so**.

Chapter 49
Travel, Trip, Way

Her first travel was to Egypt.

Her first **trip** was to Egypt.

They went on a long travel in Asia.

They went on a long **trip to** Asia.

They were very tired after their long travel - eight hours in the train.

They were very tired after their long **journey** - eight hours in the train.

How long does the way / travel to Manchester take?

How long does the **journey** to Manchester take?

The way here took them nearly three hours.

The **journey** here took them nearly three hours.

Our way to Portugal took us through France and Spain.

Our **journey** to Portugal took us through France and Spain.

On our way to Portugal, we **travelled** through France and Spain.

> The **journey** from Florence to Rome takes two hours.
>
> How was the **journey**? Was the train clean? Did it arrive on time?
>
> How was your **trip** to Venice? Where did you stay?
>
> Have a safe **journey / trip** home!
>
> I would like to **travel** around the world.
>
> My job involves a lot of **traveling**.
>
> I went to a **travel** agent
>
> On my **travels** in the Far East I met some very interesting people.

Guidelines

- **journey** - the time you spend going from A to B (flying / on the train / in the car)
- **trip** - journey + time spent in a place
- **travel** (verb) - move by transport
- **travel** (adjective) - travel agent, travel arrangements, travel time
- **travels** - not common, in any case used to refer to journeys and stays in distant places
- **on the way** - during the journey

Choose the correct form

1. They organized some **travels / trips** together.
2. I love **traveling / tripping** seeing all the different parts of the country.
3. Perhaps I was foolish to **travel / journey** alone.
4. I have to admit that I'm a bit nervous about this **trip / travel**.
5. You don't have to go on that **journey / trip** with Nicole, why not go on holiday with someone else?
6. We met a lot of traffic on the **journey / trip / way**, so we were driving really slowly.
7. What a tedious **journey / travel** you must have had.
8. Have a safe **journey / trip / way** back to Manchester.
9. If you drive during the rush hour your **travel / journey / trip** takes at least an hour longer.
10. Which country did you like the best on your **travels / trips / journeys**, my lord?
11. The **journey / trip / way** is often the best part of a holiday.
12. We've all been on a psychological **journey / trip** together, and we've met a lot of difficulties on the **way / trip**.

1) trips 2) traveling 3) travel 4) trip 5) trip 6) way 7) journey 8) journey / trip 9) journey 10) travels 11) journey 12) journey, way

Chapter 50
Understand, Catch, Figure Out, Realize

On the telephone: Sorry the line is bad. I didn't understand what you said.

On the telephone: Sorry the line is bad. I didn't quite **catch** what you said.

Many people who work in customer service don't catch the technical problems that the clients are asking about.

Many people who work in customer service don't **understand** the technical problems that the clients are asking about.

I can't realize how this thing works.

I can't **figure out / understand** how this thing works.

Until I saw her face I hadn't understood how beautiful she really was.

Until I saw her face I hadn't **realized** how beautiful she really was.

Nobody realized whether she was coming or not.

Nobody **knew** whether she was coming or not.

I am not understanding this question.

I **do not understand** this question.

Her mother realized her threat and grounded him for a week.

Her mother **carried out** her threat and grounded him for a week.

I have known that you are getting married.

I have **heard** that you are getting married.

> I did not **understand** what she said. I mean, I heard what she said but didn't understand the concept.
>
> I didn't **catch** what she said. (I didn't hear what she said, she was speaking so fast).
>
> I **realized** I had gone to the wrong house when no one answered the door.
>
> I can't **figure out** how this program works - it's very complex and there are lots of steps involved.

Guidelines

- **understand** - perceive the intended meaning / concept
- **didn't catch** - didn't understand or hear something because of the noise, or because you were distracted or not really listening
- **figure out** - understand something or find a solution after a lot of thought
- **realize / realize** - become fully aware / conscious of something

1. It wasn't until he put the camera into his bag that he **figured out / realized / understood** he was being watched by the store's security guard.
2. I'm sorry I didn't **catch / realize / understand** that. Can you say it again - I was distracted.
3. That was when I **caught / realized / understood** that she had been lying to me.
4. I've managed to **figure out / realize / understand** why my laptop wouldn't turn off.
5. No one could **catch / figure out / realize** how the robber managed to get away with all the money without anyone seeing him.
6. When we **figured out / realized / understood** how childish we'd been, we immediately said we were sorry.
7. When we finally **caught / figured out** what had been going on it was too late.
8. I still don't **catch / realize / understand** why we have to study all this - it's not even going to be in the exam.
9. I don't even **catch / realize / understand** what I'm supposed to be doing.
10. I didn't **figure out / realize / understand** you were paying such close attention.
11. She probably didn't think I'd **figure out / catch / understand**.
12. Sorry, I didn't **catch / realize / understand** your name.

1) realized 2) catch 3) realized 4) figure out 5) figure out 6) realized 7) figured out 8) understand 9) understand 10) realize 11) understand (figure it out) 12) catch

Part II
Revision Tests

Chapter 51
Revision Tests

Instructions

In this section all the sentences contain mistakes.

Find and correct the mistake.

Check your answers by referring to the relevant subsection in Part I. For example when you have corrected the sentences related to **1 according to**, go to the top of page 3 and check your answers.

Note: In some cases you will need to make corrections with words that do not appear in the chapter heading. For example, in sentence number 1 in the first exercise, you will need to replace "according to me" with "in my opinion" - "in my opinion" does not appear in the chapter heading for "according to".

1 according to

1. According to me, this will never work.
2. According to his opinion, it was my fault.
3. You must according to the doctor's advice.
4. According to the accident, she arrived late for the party.
5. According to all these reasons, we decided to abandon the project.

2 actual, actually

1. The information on the website is not actual.
2. This is a very actual question in US politics.
3. So what do you do? I am a trained account but actually I am between jobs.
4. I was born in Morocco but I actually live in Peru.
5. I moved to the now apartment last month.

3 advice, advise

1. Please can you give me one advice?
2. They gave me many good advices.
3. I advice you to visit the museum.
4. I advise to see the doctor.

4 agree

1. Are you agree with me? Yes, I am agree.
2. I am not agree with you.
3. We were both agreed that it was the right thing to do.
4. I don't agree people who vote right wing.
5. Few people agreed helping us.
6. Do you agree what he said?
7. Do you agree with my opinion?

5 among, between, of

1. Many people can't distinguish among red and green.
2. Unemployment between graduates is estimated at higher than 40%.
3. Luxembourg lies among Belgium, Germany and France
4. Tomorrow's temperature will vary between 20 to 25 degrees.
5. Next week your uncle will be among us.
6. Illiteracy is commonest under rural women.

6 appreciate

1. I would appreciate if you could make less noise.
2. The attendees appreciated the talk by applauding.
3. Their efforts should be appreciated in some way.
4. Pink Floyd are appreciated by some of my friends.

7 as vs like

1. He's acting like the manager until the real boss comes back.
2. She started to cry as a baby.
3. This Monday, as all Mondays, there will be a meeting.
4. She plays as you.
5. It looks as they won't be coming.
6. They looked as they were disappointed.
7. I prefer red fruits as strawberries and raspberries.

8 available, comfortable, convenient, ready

1. What time are you convenient?
2. She is a very available person.
3. It's very comfortable living in the center of town.
4. It is more comfortable to download them.
5. It is not convenient to do X, it is better to do Y.
6. This chair is not very comfort.
7. I hope he takes it comfortable.
8. Please be available at six to leave the hotel.

9 beautiful, good, fine, nice

1. She gets a beautiful salary.
2. It is a beautiful film - excellent plot, lots of action and a great soundtrack.
3. He is a beautiful man.
4. The most beautiful thing about this job is that I only have to work three days a week.
5. We had beautiful weather on our short holidays, just a bit of rain and few cloudy days.
6. How are you? Not very fine.
7. She studies the beautiful arts.

10 because, why

1. Because her terrible English, no one understood a word she said.
2. Because she was too young, so she couldn't watch the movies.
3. I don't see why is this man so angry.
4. She wants to make a contribution to the community therefore she does community service.
5. Why haven't you finished the homework? It is because I didn't have time.
6. Why not to do it now?
7. Why to go there when you could stay here?
8. They asked me the reason for which I had done it.
9. I did not study much. Because of it I failed the exam.

11 big, great, large

1. I paid a big amount for the tickets.
2. Your company is great enough to be considered a middle-sized company.
3. Quite a big number of people voted for Trump.
4. He has a big disease.
5. The meeting was attended by a large number of audience.
6. I have a big hunger.
7. I hope you don't think my article is too big.

12 borrow, lend, loan

1. Can I lend your pen a minute please?
2. Can you borrow me your car?
3. I borrowed my car to a friend.
4. My friend has borrowed me her bike.
5. The bank borrowed us the money.
6. Can I borrow your bathroom?

13 both, either, neither

1. Both of them didn't come to the party.
2. Both the two languages are based on Latin.
3. I don't like both of the novels. either
4. I don't speak Cantonese and Mandarin.
5. I found neither the books on Amazon.
6. In the exam you can neither talk or use a dictionary.
7. Me and my twin sister can both speak English, but we have both problems with Russian. both have
8. Neither she nor I couldn't understand a word.
9. We talked to both about the problem.

14 bring, take, carry, fetch, get, lead

1. An ambulance carried the victim to the hospital.
2. Shall I bring you home?
3. She brought the baby to bed. put
4. They brought a political debate on TV last night. broadcast, showed
5. We're going to the USA and want to bring medicines with us.

15 camping, campsite, parking, car park

1. On holidays we often go to camping.
2. Next weekend we shall have a camping.
3. There are four or five campings along the coast.
4. There is a parking near the supermarket.
5. I couldn't find a parking that's why I am late.

16 chance, possibility, occasion

1. There is an opportunity that she will come tonight.
2. Doing the Erasmus gave me my first occasion to travel abroad.
3. Is there any possibility of me borrowing your laptop? chance
4. This new situation opens up all kinds of chances.
5. There is no possibility to control her thoughts.
6. They had the possibility to help us.
7. We had not other possibilities but to go.
8. The more qualified you are the greater the chances to find a job.

17 close, near, next

1. I have a flat in the near of the university.
2. I hope to travel round Asia in the next time / in the coming future.
3. It's in the near.
4. There a lot of hills nearby Florence.
5. We came near to a solution.
6. We went to the near town of Lucca.
7. Where is the next bank?
8. I was standing at the bus stop and he came near me.

18 clothes, dress, dresses, get dressed, put on, wear

1. The boys need some new dresses.
2. If they like to wear like that, then who are we to say they shouldn't?
3. Do you follow any rules when you wear in the morning?
4. My three year old child cannot dress by himself
5. Do I have to carry a tie? wear
6. I get up and immediately wear my clothes.
7. Most of the police force wear guns.

19 come, go

1. My horrible aunt was staying with us so I didn't want to come back home.
2. I prefer to come back to / return to my house on foot.
3. People coming from Asia are often stereotyped as being good at math.
4. If I don't go now I won't come before it goes dark.
5. Sorry but we've only just opened and Ms Wang hasn't come back yet.
6. The baby is just learning to go.
7. When does the next bus go?
8. When I back to Kobe it was already dark

20 control, check

1. They controlled our luggage at the customs.
2. Have you controlled what time the train leaves?
3. Did you control the translation yet?
4. They use a hidden camera to control their children.
5. I am not sure where she is but I don't control her all the time.

21 cook, cooker, cooking, kitchen, dish, course, plate

1. If you don't like the food don't blame me I am not the cooker.
2. I prefer Italian kitchen.
3. They serve only traditional plates from the region.
4. What are we having for the main dish / plate?

22 do, make

1. I mistake. / I did a mistake
2. I am making a course on French cuisine.
3. I am making my driving test next week.
4. I want to make my PhD in Sweden.
5. I make you a photo.
6. Tell me about some of the experiences you made while you were in Peru.
7. When do you usually make your holidays? take / have
8. I'm going to make an eye test.

23 early, soon, on time, in time

1. I hope to see you early - let me know when would suit you.
2. I hope we've not come too soon - I know it's only 7 o'clock but we were so excited about coming.
3. The buses on this route never arrive in time.

24 earn, gain, win, beat, deserve

1. She won me easily at tennis.
2. I have deserved the respect of my students.
3. She has a good job and wins a lot of money.
4. They didn't earn to win.
5. At school I learned a lot of knowledge.

25 economic, economical, economically, financial

1. Our economical situation is bad, neither of us has any money.
2. The company's economic report is due at the end of the month.
3. The economical situation in our country is very bad.
4. The economical crisis is killing the country.
5. This car is economic because it does 200 km per liter.

26 education, background, upbringing, (good/bad) manners, training

1. They believe she is a criminal because of her bad education.
2. A person's genes and their education are two different things.
3. He decided there was no necessity for continuous formation.
4. I had a training last week.
5. This formation involves a lot of theoretical knowledge.
6. The fact that he has no education is clear - look at the way he behaves on social occasions.

27 enjoy, have a good time, funny, fun

1. We studied very hard but we were enjoying.
2. I wanted to find a hobby that enjoyed me.
3. I enjoy to watch football.
4. Going to the beach is always funny.
5. It's not fun being around you.
6. It's not funny being the manager - you have to reprimand people all day.

28 enough, quite, pretty, sufficient

1. The time is not enough for us to finish this job.
2. They didn't have enough time to finish the exercise.
3. We didn't take enough of food with us.
4. The movie was enough good.
5. One advantage of RyanAir and EasyJet is that they cheap enough.
6. This year school is quite harder than last year.

29 even if, even though, although

1. Even if it was really hot they wore a coat.
2. Her English is not very good even she has studied it for ten years.
3. I prefer red wine to white wine, even if I enjoy white wine too.
4. Although it was raining, but we still went on the picnic.

30 ever, never, always

1. What about this movie? Have you never seen it? It's really great, I think you'd love it.
2. He was the worst teacher that I had never had.
3. He was the worst teacher that I had ever had before.
4. She has ever been my true love.
5. Taxi drivers always don't know how much they are going to earn.
6. I am very interested in Japanese but I was never in Japan.

31 expect, wait (for)

1. At the end of her story she expected their reaction.
2. I'm waiting for an email from them to tell me whether I got the job or not.
3. We took our seats and expected the teacher to come.
4. I expected her outside the cinema but she never came
5. I am waiting him at 8 - we have an appointment.
6. I expect myself that he will be late.

32 find, find out, discover, search, look for

1. Can you find what is wrong with my PC, it keeps crashing?
2. Look on the web I found out some interesting sites.
3. In the movie he finds out a means to convert iron into gold.
4. I have to search my keys every time I leave the house.
5. He was looking desperately for something to say. searching
6. She hasn't started yet, she's still finding her book.
7. I am looking for the truth.
8. I am finding very difficult to learn Chinese.
9. (On the phone) I am looking for Adrian.

33 fit, match, suit, go well with

1. Red is a color that fits me very well.
2. The jacket doesn't match the shirt.
3. This wine is great but it doesn't fit well with white meat.

34 grow, grow up, increase, cultivate

1. Many children grow in an atmosphere of violence.
2. We need to go back to the time when mothers stayed at home growing children.
3. My mother was grown in Warsaw.
4. Our olive oil production grows every year.

35 happen, occur, take place

1. The seminar will occur at 09.00 tomorrow.
2. A fire happened at the school over the weekend.
3. An accident was happened outside my house.
4. Did there happen something strange?
5. It happened / succeeded the same thing to me.
6. What has happened with you?
7. It may happen that I get drunk at parties.
8. The art historians thought it was a Van Gogh, but it occurred that it was a fake. What we occur to overcome this challenge is a new strategy.

36 home, house; homework, housework

1. Our home is next door to a cinema.
2. When I returned to house I found that the door had been broken.
3. His house is an apartment.
4. When I arrived at home I had a shower.
5. We don't have any time to do the home work so we have hired a cleaner.
6. Don't give us too many homeworks.

37 in the end, at the end, eventually, finally, at last, lastly, if necessary

1. At the end there was nothing we could do about it. We'd tried everything.
2. They came at the end having made me wait nearly three hours.
3. At last, I want to say that ...
4. First we listened to some music, then we watched a move, and at last we went to bed.
5. He comes eventually.
6. Some viewers may find the movie eventually shocking.
7. Stop crying at last and tell me what happened.

38 job, work

1. She has two works - a mother and a housewife.
2. This is a work for an expert.
3. This will take a long time - it's a hard work.
4. The company has created 10 new workplaces.
5. I must do a work for my English teacher.
6. She is employed in the same company as him.

39 know, meet

1. I have known him at a party.
2. He wants to travel so that he can know other people.
3. By working in an office, you know a lot of people.
4. She didn't go in the sea, because she didn't know swimming.
5. The best way to know a city is to visit it on foot.
6. At the party I knew many new friends.
7. I have known you are leaving soon - I am really sorry.
8. I don't know English very well.

40 last, latest, most recent; next, the next

1. Have you read his last novel?
2. The latest election was won by the Republicans.
3. She arrived the last week.
4. I didn't sleep well this night.
5. Last evening we went to the movies. yesterday
6. On last Saturday we went to the movies.
7. In the last time houses prices have been going up dramatically.
8. I am very busy in this period / in these days.

41 look at, see, watch

1. We looked at a movie on Netflix.
2. We spent the day watching paintings at the modern art museum.
3. She had a quick look on her watch and decided to leave.
4. I don't face to face with my neighbors.
5. When I was young I liked watching comics.
6. You see pale today.
7. Have you seen our tests yet?

42 look, seem, sound

1. It looks a good idea.
2. He looks an English man.
3. You look like nervous.
4. I heard a noise that sounded to be a child crying.
5. Your house looks wonderfully.
6. My accent in English doesn't sound well.

43 lose, lack, miss, waste

1. I don't want to lose any more time doing this stupid exercise.
2. He misses intelligence.
3. In emails the tone of voice is missing.
4. Have you finished the test? I am missing the last question.
5. She has three exams missing.
6. I was missing at the last lesson.
7. I have to loose weight / to lose my weight.
8. Our country lacks of care for the homeless.

44 remember, remind, forget

1. I remind the holidays we spent together.
2. I don't want to be remembered that it is my birthday today.
3. I would like to remember you that we need the doc by the end of this week.
4. I did not remember to meet them before, but I pretended I knew them.
5. As I remember, you prefer red wine to white.
6. I suddenly memorized that I had a dentist's appointment.
7. He forgot his homework at home.
8. Buy now - they will probably rise the cost of the seats as the holidays gets closer.

45 rise, arise, raise

1. The sun raises in the east.
2. I am hoping my boss will rise my salary.
3. My salary has not raised with inflation
4. A problem has rised.

46 say, tell

1. Can you say me where the station is?
2. He told: "I love you"
3. I said her that I loved her
4. Please tell Anna "hello".
5. She told that the movie was not very good.
6. I was said to report to you for instructions.
7. Do we have to say about what we think?

47 sorry, excuse, apologize

1. He asked the teacher if he could be pardoned for a few minutes while he made a phone call.
2. I apologized myself for being late.
3. I really sorry about what happened.
4. Could you excuse me at the meeting tomorrow?

48 think, think of, think about, believe

1. A: She will come. B: I believe that too.
2. I believed she was a police officer.
3. What do you think about? I am thinking to my mother.
4. Do you believe that they will come?
5. I am thinking to go to Thailand.
6. I think he didn't understand.
7. If you mean nothing is impossible, try getting a ticket to Adele's concert. think
8. In my opinion, I think you should see a doctor.

49 travel, trip, transport, way

1. Her first travel was to Egypt.
2. They went on a long travel in Asia.
3. They were very tired after their long travel - eight hours in the train.
4. How long does the way / travel to Manchester take?
5. The way here took them nearly three hours.
6. Our way to Portugal took us through France and Spain.

50 understand, catch, figure out, realize

1. On the telephone: Sorry the line is bad. I didn't understand what you said.
2. Many people who work in customer service don't catch the technical problems that the clients are asking about.
3. I can't how this thing works.
4. Until I saw her face I hadn't understood how beautiful she really was.
5. Nobody realized whether she was coming or not.
6. I am not understanding this question.
7. Her mother realized her threat and grounded him for a week.
8. I have known that you are getting married.

Part III
False Friends

Chapter 52
False Friends

Top 50 False Friends

A false friend is a word in one's own language that looks the same as word in another language but has in fact a different meaning.

The ones in bold are dealt with in Part I of this book in the sections given in brackets.

		MEANS	DOES NOT MEAN
1.	accurate	correct in all details	tidy, smart; thorough
2.	**actually** (2)	really, in reality	currently, at the moment
3.	agenda	list of things to discuss	diary, note book
4.	argument	heated discussion	subject, topic
5.	assist	help	attend, participate, be present
6.	camera	device for taking photographs	room, cell, chamber
7.	**camping** (15)	the act of camping	campsite
8.	canteen	work cafeteria	cellar
9.	**comfortable** (8)	allowing one to relax	convenient
10.	**convenient** (8)	suitable, situated nearby	inexpensive
11.	**control** (20)	exert power, regulate	check, verify
12.	deception	makes someone believe something else	disappointment
13.	**education** (26)	what you learn at school	upbringing (what you learn at home)
14.	embarrassed	feel uncomfortable	pregnant
15.	**eventually** (37)	in the end (after some trouble)	if necessary, in the likely course of events

#	Word	Meaning	Alternative
16.	fabric	cloth, material	factory
17.	feminist	supporting male / female equality	man who pampers women
18.	genial	friendly	brilliant
19.	gymnasium	facility for sports and exercise (gym)	school
20.	history	the events of a country	the events in a work of fiction
21.	journal	a weekly or monthly magazine	a daily newspaper
22.	lecture	a talk giving information	a reading text
23.	library	a place for borrowing books	a place for buying books
24.	local	an adjective meaning near	a pub, night club
25.	lucky	fortunate	happy
26.	magazine	a weekly publication	a store house or warehouse
27.	manifestation	giving a clear example	demonstration
28.	material	fabric, cloth, facts, substance	a subject studied
29.	novel	a book of fiction	a short story
30.	obligation	something you have to do	financial instrument
31.	parents	mother and father	relatives
32.	pathetic	very inadequate, arousing pity	pompous, sensitive, liable to suffer
33.	photograph	picture	photographer
34.	physicist	someone who studies physics	doctor, physician
35.	possibly	if possible	perhaps, please
36.	preservative	substance used to preserve food	condom
37.	pretend	fake, claim	expect, intend, aspire to
38.	professor	university academic	school teacher
39.	propaganda	false publicity for political aims	advertising
40.	proper	correct, suitable, right	own
41.	public	people in general	audience, spectators
42.	**realize** (50)	begin to understand	create, develop
43.	regard	be related to	look at
44.	receipt	proof of purchase	recipe (food), prescription (medicine)
45.	sensible	reasonable, practical	sensitive
46.	serious	not humorous	professional
47.	smoking	the act of smoking	a (smoking) jacket
48.	sympathetic	understanding of other's situation	friendly, nice, easy to get on with
49.	technique	method	technology
50.	voyage	journey by sea or space	any kind of journey

Exercises on False Friends

1

Insert an appropriate word from the box below. Note: You will not need all the words.

1. My _____ and I are going to _____ an international conference next month in Beijing. The various papers that are presented will then be published in a scientific _____ .
2. This 300 page historical _____ shows how for much of its _____ , Finland has been a battleground for fights between Sweden and Russia.
3. I am a fashion designer and I use all types of _____ in my creations. Actually, there is an interview with me in a fashion _____ that should be available next month.
4. They emailed me the _____ for tomorrow's meeting.
5. This painting is an abstract _____ of how I see Europe.
6. He is a _____ and is giving a _____ at Harvard University on a new cure for cancer.

> agenda, assist, attend, diary, history, lecture, manifestation, materials, novel, physicist, physician, professor, short story, teacher, warehouse,

1. My **professor** and I are going to **attend** an international conference next month in Beijing. The various papers that are presented will then be published in a scientific **journal**.
2. This 300 page historical **novel** shows how for much of its **history**, Finland has been a battleground for fights between Sweden and Russia.
3. I am a fashion designer and I use all types of **materials** in my creations. Actually, there is an interview with me in a fashion **magazine** that should be available next month.
4. They emailed me the **agenda** for tomorrow's meeting.
5. This painting is an abstract **manifestation** of how I see Europe.
6. He is a **physician** and is giving a **lecture** at Harvard University on a new cure for cancer.

2

Insert an appropriate word from the box below. Note: You will not need all the words.

1. You have done a very _____ translation - I can't find any mistakes. I think it was very sensible of you not to have done a too _____ translation. In fact you seem to have really caught the essence of the original.
2. She is a _____ and works with a _____ group to try and get the community to really understand the obstacles that women still have today in the workplace and also in society in general.
3. I know it was pretty _____ of me to get _____ about something so insignificant, particularly given the _____ nature of the people I was dealing with.
4. I would be good to meet up, _____ next week.
5. She is very _____ , doesn't laugh much. She always ensures that everything is done in the _____ way - she really sticks to the regulations.
6. He is so _____ - he won the lottery twice in the same year.

> accurate, brilliant, embarrassed, feminist, genial, happy, literal, local, lucky, night club, pathetic, possibly, proper, sensitive, serious

1. You have done a very **accurate** translation - I can't find any mistakes. I think it was very **sensible** of you not to have done a too **literal** translation. In fact you seem to have really caught the essence of the original.
2. She is a **feminist** and works with a **local** group to try and get the community to really understand the obstacles that women still have today in the workplace and also in society in general.
3. I know it was pretty **pathetic** of me to get **embarrassed** about something so insignificant, particularly given the **genial** nature of the people I was dealing with.
4. I would be good to meet up, **possibly** next week.
5. She is very **serious**, doesn't laugh much. She always ensures that everything is done in the **proper** way - she really sticks to the regulations.
6. He is so **lucky** - he won the lottery twice in the same year.

3

Insert an appropriate word from the box below. Note: You will not need all the words.

1. I took the _____ with a new Sony _____ that I have just bought, using a _____ that I learned during a photography course.
2. _____ is not allowed in the work _____ .
3. The right wing parties tend to release a lot of _____ that _____ misinformation on immigration in order to promote their racist agenda. It is a well organized process of _____ .
4. He works in a _____ that produces _____ for the food industry.
5. He _____ that when he was young he had been on _____ across the Atlantic with his _____ . In reality only his mother had been with him, not his father.
6. You have an _____ to produce a _____ if you want a refund.

> advertising, camera, canteen, deception, fabric, factory, obligation, parents, photograph, preservatives, pretended, propaganda, receipt, recipe, regards, relatives, smoking, technique, technology, voyage

1. I took the **photograph** with a new Sony **camera** that I have just bought, using a **technique** that I learned during a photography course.
2. **Smoking** is not allowed in the work **canteen**.
3. The right wing parties tend to release a lot of **propaganda** that **regards** misinformation on immigration in order to promote their racist agenda. It is a well organized process of **deception**.
4. He works in a **factory** that produces **preservatives** for the food industry.
5. He **pretended** that when he was young he had been on **voyage** across the Atlantic with his **parents**. In reality only his mother had been with him, not his father.
6. You have an **obligation** to produce a **receipt** if you want a refund.

4

Underline the correct synonym for the word in the first column.

For the ones in italics you will need to consult a good dictionary (e.g. Word Reference) as they are not listed in the top 50 False Friends.

1. actually — currently / at the moment / in reality
2. argument — heated discussion / subject / topic / issue
3. *advertisement* — warning / publicity
4. *comprehensive* — exhaustive / understanding / sympathetic
5. consistent — substantial / in line with everything else
6. convenient — good value / a good idea
7. educated — with a good cultural background / polite
8. eventually — in the end / if necessary
9. *impressed* — shocked / horrified / pleasantly surprised
10. library — where books can be borrowed / where books can be bought
11. *occasion* — opportunity / a particular moment
12. *occur* — to need / to take place
13. possibly — perhaps / if possible
14. sympathetic — friendly / good fun / nice / understanding

1) in reality 2) heated discussion 3) publicity 4) exhaustive 5) in line with everything else 6) a good idea 7) with a good cultural background 8) in the end 9) pleasantly surprised 10) where books can be borrowed 11) a particular moment 12) to take place 13) perhaps 14) understanding

Appendix

Below are the indexes to two other books containing grammar and vocabulary exercises. If you are a student, you can use these indexes to find additional exercises. You can also use the link below to take you to you to English for Academic Research: Grammar, Usage and Style where you can find more detailed explanations to clarify certain difficulties connected to grammar and vocabulary:

http://www.springer.com/gp/book/9781461415923

English for Academic Research: Grammar Exercises Index

This index is by section number. Numbers marked in bold mean that the whole section

a few vs *few* 4.4, 4.5
a little vs *little* 4.4, 4.5
a vs *an* 3.1, 3.2, 18.1
a/an vs *one* 3.2
abbreviations 17.2
able to 12.7
abstracts - grammar **19, 25**
acknowledgements - tenses **23**
acronyms 17.1
active form **10**, 20.3, 21.2, 21.3, 22.3, 26.2
adjectives - position 14.3
adverbs - position 14.7-14.14
adverbs of frequency - position 14.7
adverbs of manner - position 14.8
allow 11.4, 11.5
allowed to 12.11
also - position 14.11

any, some and derivatives 4.1, 4.2, 4.3
articles (definite, indefinite, zero) **3**,18.1
be able to 12.7
be allowed to 12.11
be supposed to 12.11
be vs *have* 10.1
both - position 14.11
can 12.1, 12.2, 12.3, 12.7, 12.8, 23.4, 23.5
clearly - position 14.10
commas in relative clauses 5.5, 5.6
comparative form **15**, position 14.3
conclusions - tenses **24, 25**
conditional forms **9**
consistently - position 14.10
could 12.4, 12.5, 12.6, 12.7, 12.8, 23.4, 23.5
countable vs uncountable nouns 1.2, 1.3, 1.4
defining vs non defining relative clauses **5**

definite article (*the*) **3**,18.2, 18.3, 22.1. 22.2
direct object - position 14.2, 14.5, 14.6
discussion - tenses **23**
either - position 14.11
enable 11.4, 11.5
few vs *a few* 4.4, 4.5
finally - position 14.10
first conditional 9.1, 9.2, 9.4, 9.5
future continuous 8.4, 8.5
future simple (*will*) **8**
genitive **2**
gerund (*-ing* form) **11**
going to 8.2, 8.3
have to 12.9, 12.10, 12.11
have vs *be* 10.1
hypotheses **9**, 23.1
indefinite article (*a/an*) **3**,18.1-18.3, 22.2
indirect object - position 14.2
infinitive **11**
-ing form **11**
introduction - tenses **20**
inversion of subject and object 14.5, 14.6
just - position 14.9
little vs *a little* 4.4, 4.5
lots 4.5
many 4.5
may 12.1, 12.2, 12.3, 12.7, 12.8, 23.4, 23.5
methods - tenses **21**
might 12.4, 12.5, 12.6, 23.4, 23.5
modal verbs 9.7-9.9, **12**, 23.4, 23.5, 24.5
the more ... the more 15.2
much 4.5
must 12.8, 12.9, 12.10, 12.11
normally - position 14.10
noun verb agreement 1.1
nouns: countable vs uncountable 1.2, 1.3, 1.4
numbers **16**
one vs *a/an* 3.2
passive form **10**, 20.3, 21.2, 21.3, 22.3, 26.2
past continuous 7.7, 7.8, 7.9
past participle - position 14.4
past perfect 7.6, 7.8, 7.9
past simple **7**, **19**, 20.1, 20.2, 20.4, 20.5, 20.6, 21.4, 22.4, 23.2, 23.3, 23.6
permit 11.4, 11.5
phrasal verbs **13**
prefer 11.6
prepositions in titles 18.4
present continuous 6.1, 6.2, 6.3, 19.7

present perfect 6.2, 6.3, 6.4, 7.1-7.5, 19.3, 20.1, 20.2, 20.4, 20.5, 20.6, 21.4, 22.4, 23.3, 23.6
present perfect continuous 6.3, 6.4, 7.4, 7.5,
present simple 6.1, 6.2, 6.3, 8.1, **19**, 20.1, 20.2, 20.6, 21.4, 22.4, 23.2, 23.3, 23.6
present tenses **6**
quantifiers **4**
questions - word order 14.5
recommend 11.6
relative pronouns **5**
results - tenses **22**
review of the literature - tenses **20**
second conditional 9.2, 9.3, 9.4, 9.5
shall 8.6
should 9.7, 9.8, 9.9, 12.11, 21.1
some, any and derivatives 4.1, 4.2, 4.3
structured abstract - tenses 19.5, 19.6
subject - position 14.1, 14.5, 14.6
suggest 11.6
superlative form **15**
supposed to 12.11
syntax **14**
tenses: present **6**, past **7**, future **8**
that **5**
the more ... the more 15.2
third conditional 9.3, 9.4, 9.5, 20.6
titles - grammar **18**
uncountable vs countable nouns 1.2, 1.3, 1.4
verb noun agreement 1.1
verbs - phrasal **13**
want 11.6
what 5.7, 5.8
which **5**
which vs *what* 5.7, 5.8
who **5**
whose 5.4
will **8**, 12.7
will vs *going to* 8.2, 8.3
word order **14**
would - conditional form **9**
would - future in the past 20.7, 21.1, 23.2
would have to vs *should* 9.7
would like 9.6, 11.6
would vs *should* 9.8, 9.9
would vs *would like* 9.6
zero article **3**,18.2, 18.3, 22.2
zero conditional 9.1, 9.4, 9.5

English for Academic Research: Vocabulary Exercises

This table of contents refers to the chapter numbers.

Section 1 Adjectives and Adverbs

1.1 actual, current, topical
1.2 actually, currently, nowadays
1.3 advisable, convenient, comfortable
1.4 all, entire, everything, whole
1.5 almost, hard, hardly, nearly
1.6 alone, only, solely
1.7 alone, individual, only, single, sole, unique
1.8 alternate(ly), alternative(ly)
1.9 always, ever, never
1.10 apparently, seemingly
1.11 appropriate, proper, right, suitable
1.12 appropriate(ly), convenient(ly), correct(ly), proper(ly), right (ly)
1.13 at present, currently, now, nowadays
1.14 characteristic, peculiar, typical, unique
1.15 classic, classical
1.16 coherent(ly), consistent(ly)
1.17 coherent(ly), consistent(ly), substantial(ly)
1.18 common, diffuse, widespread
1.19 comprehensible, understandable
1.20 connected, linked, related
1.21 contemporary, contemporaneous, simultaneous
1.22 continual(ly), continuous(ly)
1.23 corresponding, correspondent
1.24 deeply, strictly, strongly, tightly, thoroughly
1.25 different, several, various
1.26 each, every, any
1.27 each other, one another, themselves
1.28 early, soon
1.29 economic, economical, economically, financial
1.30 economic, low-cost
1.31 enough, quite, sufficient(ly)
1.32 few, little, a few, a little
1.33 fewer, less, minor
1.34 for, since
1.35 greater, main, major
1.36 independent(ly), irrespective(ly), regardless(ly)
1.37 main, principal, principle
1.38 pointless, useless
1.39 relevant, remarkable, significant
1.40 sensible, sensitive
1.41 subsequent(ly), successive(ly)
1.42 adverbs of manner 1
1.43 adverbs of manner 2
1.44 adverbs of time
1.45 adjectives -*ing* vs -*ed*
1.46 adjectives
1.47 adjectives: positive and negative
1.48 adjectives with similar meanings

Section 2 Link words

2.1 according to, depending on, following, in accordance with, in agreement with, in compliance with,
2.2 also, as well as, even, too
2.3 also, as well as, either, even, neither/nor, not only, so, too
2.4 although, even if, even though, though
2.5 apart from, besides, except for, in addition to, with the exception of
2.6 as long as, if, provided that, unless
2.7 as is, as it is
2.8 as, how, like
2.9 as a consequence, consequently, hence, it follows that, thus, therefore
2.10 at the end, in the end, finally, lastly
2.11 because, why
2.12 both, either, neither
2.13 both, either, neither, if, whether
2.14 by now, for the moment, so far

2.15 by, thus, when, while
2.16 compared to, in relation to, with respect to
2.17 despite, despite the fact, however, in any case, in spite of the fact, nevertheless, notwithstanding, still, yet
2.18 e.g., i.e.
2.19 e.g., for example, i.e., such as, that is to say, etc
2.20 eventual(ly), if necessary, in the end
2.21 in fact, instead (of), on the other contrary, on the other hand
2.22 Various link words 1
2.23 Various link words 2

Section 3 Nouns

3.1 base, basis
3.2 basis, degree, extent, level, region
3.3 capacity, competence, skill
3.4 chance, opportunity, possibility, probability
3.5 consideration, observation, remark
3.6 danger, hazard
3.7 dimension, size
3.8 measure, measurement
3.9 motivation, reason
3.10 replacement, substitute, substitution
3.11 requirement, request, query
3.12 Various nouns

Section 4 Prepositions

4.1 about, for, of
4.2 above, over, below, under, underneath
4.3 among, between, of
4.4 among, between, from, of, with
4.5 at, in, into, inside, to
4.6 at, to, Ø (no preposition)
4.7 at, to, towards
4.8 by, from
4.9 by, from, in, of, with
4.10 during, over, throughout
4.11 for, of
4.12 in, into
4.13 in, on
4.14 in, into, on, onto
4.15 with, within

Section 5 Verbs

5.1 affect, effect, influence, condition, interest
5.2 agree with, be in agreement with, match
5.3 allow, enable, permit, let, mean
5.4 analyze, elaborate, process
5.5 anticipate, bring forward, expect, forecast, foresee, predict
5.6 argue, claim, pretend
5.7 arise, raise, rise, lead to
5.8 ascertain, check, control, verify
5.9 assist, take part, participate
5.10 assume, hypothesize, suppose
5.11 assure, ensure, guarantee, insure
5.12 attempt, demonstrate, prove, show, test, try, try out
5.13 avoid, prevent
5.14 be concerned, cope with, deal with, focus on
5.15 be the result of, turn out, result, result in
5.16 be born, conceive, derive from, originate
5.17 bind, bond, bound
5.18 bring, cause, determine, give rise to, lead to
5.19 compose, comprise, consist, constitute, form, make up
5.20 condition, conduct, drive, guide
5.21 decline, decrease, go down, lessen, lower, reduce
5.22 degree, grade, level
5.23 demand, request, require, requirement
5.24 desire, want, wish
5.25 determine, cause, induce, lead to
5.26 depict, highlight, show, visualize
5.27 detect, discriminate, distinguish, identify
5.28 divide, separate, share, split
5.29 entail, imply, involve, mean
5.30 evidence, highlight, show
5.31 exclude, rule out, marginalize
5.32 expect, presume, suppose, wait for
5.33 experiment, experience, proof, prove, test
5.34 lack, miss

5.35 propose, recommend, suggest
5.36 refuse, reject
5.37 replace, substitute
5.38 result, turn out
5.39 review, revise, revisit
5.40 subject to, subjected to, undergo
5.41 Irregular verbs
5.42 Phrasal Verbs 1
5.43 Phrasal Verbs 2
5.44 Phrasal Verbs 3

Section 6 False Friends and Synonyms

6.1 False friends 1
6.2 False friends 2
6.3 Synonyms 1: reducing redundancy
6.4 Synonyms: Latinate vs Anglo Saxon 1
6.5 Synonyms: Latinate vs Anglo Saxon 2
6.6 Various Synonyms

Index

A
according to, 1
actual, 2
actually, 2
advice, 3
agree, 4
although, 29
always, 30
among, 5
apologize, 47
appreciate, 6
arise, 45
as, 7
at last, 37
at the end, 37
available, 8

B
background, 26
beat, 27
beautiful, 9
because, 10
believe, 48
between, 5
big, 11
borrow, 12
both, 13
bring, 14

C
camping, 15
campsite, 15
car park, 15
carry, 14
catch, 50
chance, 16
check, 20
close, 17
clothes, 18
come, 19
comfortable, 8
control, 20
convenient, 8
cook, 21
cooker, 21
cooking, 21
course, 21
cultivate, 34

D
deserve, 28
discover, 32
dish, 21
do, 22
dress, 18
dresses, 18

E
early, 23
earn, 24
economic, 25
economical, 25
economically, 25
education, 26

The numbers refer to the sections in the books (not to the page numbers).

either, 13
enjoy, 27
enough, 28
even if, 29
even though, 29
eventually, 37
ever, 30
excuse, 47
expect, 31

F
fetch, 14
figure out, 50
finally, 37
financial, 25
find, 32
find out, 32
fine, 9
fit, 33
forget, 44
fun, 27
funny, 27

G
gain, 25
get, 14
get dressed, 18
go, 19
go well with, 33
good, 9
good time, have a, 27
great, 11
grow, 34
grow up, 34

H
happen, 35
have a good time, 27
home, 36
homework, 36
house, 36
housework, 36

I
if necessary, 37
in the end, 37
in time, 23
increase, 34

J
job, 38

K
kitchen, 21
know, 39

L
lack, 43
large, 11
last, 40
lastly, 37
latest, 40
lead, 14
lend, 12
like, 7
loan, 12
look, 42
look at, 41
look for
lose, 43

M
make, 22
manners, 26
match, 33
meet, 39
miss, 43
most recent, 40

N
near, 17
neither, 13
never, 30
next, 17, 40
nice, 9

O
occasion, 16
occur, 35
of, 5
on time, 23

P
parking, 15
plate, 21

possibility, 16
pretty, 28
put on, 18

Q
quite, 28

R
raise, 45
ready, 8
realize, 50
remember, 44
remind, 44
rise, 45

S
say, 46
search, 32
see, 41
seem, 42
soon, 23
sorry, 47
sound, 42
sufficient, 28
suit, 33

T
take, 14
take place, 35
tell, 46
the next, 40
think, 48
think about, 48
think of, 48
training, 26
travel, 49
trip, 49

U
understand, 50
upbringing, 26

W
wait (for) 31
waste, 43
watch, 41
way, 49
wear, 18
why, 10
win, 26
work, 38

GPSR Compliance
The European Union's (EU) General Product Safety Regulation (GPSR) is a set of rules that requires consumer products to be safe and our obligations to ensure this.

If you have any concerns about our products, you can contact us on

ProductSafety@springernature.com

In case Publisher is established outside the EU, the EU authorized representative is:

Springer Nature Customer Service Center GmbH
Europaplatz 3
69115 Heidelberg, Germany

www.ingramcontent.com/pod-product-compliance
Lightning Source LLC
LaVergne TN
LVHW010342260326
834688LV00036B/829